I0605662

ANGRY GIRLS WILL GET US THROUGH

REBECCA TRAISTER

Adapted by RUBY SHAMIR

Simon & Schuster Books for Young Readers
NEW YORK AMSTERDAM/ANTWERP LONDON
TORONTO SYDNEY/MELBOURNE NEW DELHI

SIMON & SCHUSTER BFYR

SIMON & SCHUSTER BOOKS FOR YOUNG READERS
An imprint of Simon & Schuster Children's Publishing Division
1230 Avenue of the Americas, New York, New York 10020

This young readers edition adapts material from several books by Rebecca Traister, including *Good and Mad* (Simon & Schuster, 2018), *All the Single Ladies* (Simon & Schuster, 2016), and *Big Girls Don't Cry* (Simon & Schuster, 2010).

Back cover texture by Queso/iStock
Jacket design by Sarah Creech

Interior design by Tom Daly
The text for this book was set in EB Garamond.
Manufactured in the United States of America
0126 BVG
First Edition
2 4 6 8 10 9 7 5 3 1
CIP data for this book is available from the Library of Congress.
ISBN 9781665943352
ISBN 9781665943376 (ebook)

To the girls who come after

Do not put such unlimited power into the hands of the husbands. Remember, all men would be tyrants if they could. If particular care and attention is not paid to the ladies, we are determined to foment a rebellion, and will not hold ourselves bound by any laws in which we have no voice or representation.

—Abigail Adams

Contents

ANGRY GIRLS WILL GET US THROUGH

Introduction

On February 14, 2018, a gunman who had stalked an ex-girlfriend shot and killed seventeen people at Marjory Stoneman Douglas High School in Parkland, Florida. Almost immediately after the tragedy, a group of high school students, the young people who'd survived the mass shooting, began their own campaign to end gun violence and take on the National Rifle Association (NRA). The NRA represents gun manufacturers and funnels donations into lawmakers' political campaigns to get them to oppose any restrictions on guns. Perhaps the most furious of the teenagers was eighteen-year-old Cuban American X González (who is nonbinary but identified as female at the time), who wiped away their tears and bellowed into a microphone, "The people in the government who were voted into power are lying to us. . . . Politicians who sit in their gilded House and Senate seats funded by the NRA telling us nothing could have been done to prevent this; *we call BS*." In another outburst, González's classmate Sarah Chadwick let loose some expletives on social media directed at the president at the time, Donald Trump. She later apologized for using profanity, but went on: "I'm a grieving sixteen-year-old girl who lost friends, teachers, and peers yesterday. I was and am still angry. I am apologizing for my comment but not for my anger."

Watching González, Chadwick, and their fellow students flash their fury without apology, and then use that anger to fuel a movement to try to loosen the grip of gun companies on American politicians was startling. And thrilling. It occurred to me that in the United States, we have rarely been taught how rebellious, insistent, and furious women, girls, gender-fluid people, and nonbinary people have shaped our history and our present, our activism and our art. We should be. This realization was part of what inspired me to write a book about the women, girls, and gender nonconformists who helped mold this country through their fury.

Though you will see emotions expressed colorfully on the pages that follow, this book is not an exploration of women's ire, fury, frustration, wrath, indignation, rage, or any other synonym for anger as emotion. Rather, it is about the specific link between anger and American *politics*, about how the particular dissatisfactions and resentments of America's women and girls have often ignited movements for social change and progress. It is an examination of how an impulse that many women have taken pains to hide or disguise or distance themselves from—the impulse to get *really* mad—has been crucial in determining their political power and social standing, how women's rage has played parts in revolutionary social movements, and how it has shaped the way women, including women who are leaders, activists, artists, and political candidates, have been received.

The poet June Jordan wrote a tender chronicle of rage at having her liberties restricted "because I am the wrong sex, the wrong age, the wrong skin." In *A Place of Rage*, a 1991 documentary about

Black women activists and artists, she recalled the event that shaped her approach to politics. In her childhood in Brooklyn, New York, a young man in her neighborhood was beaten on his roof by the police in a case of mistaken identity. "To see this boy I idolized, who belonged to us, in the sense of our block . . . disfigured by these strangers who came in with all this force and license to use that force was really terrifying. And also it hardened me early on in a kind of place of rage." Out of Jordan's rage came her art, and art is among the forces that reshape our world.

Our nation has been transformed by women's anger in response to all forms of prejudice and discrimination: sexism against women, racism against people of color, homophobia and transphobia against people in the LGBTQ+ community. Women's anger has pushed up against the excesses of capitalism—the American economic system in which companies exploit workers for profit—and classism—which discriminates against the poor and enables the wealthiest to take advantage of working people. Women's anger ignited fights for policies to make our world cleaner, greener, healthier, safer, smarter, more kind, and more fair. Women's anger helped abolish slavery and enfranchise women and people of color with voting rights. It has fueled feminist movements for women's equal rights and independence, in opposition to a patriarchal system in which women are ruled by men.

Even so, women's anger most often has been received and defined as negative: often vilified as evil and ugly, or marginalized as ineffective or useless. Black women's fury is treated differently from white women's rage; poor women's frustrations are heard differently from the ire of the wealthy. Yet despite the varied and unjust ways America has dismissed or ridiculed the rages of women, those rages have often created real, practical change to the nation's rules and practices and customs, to its very fabric. In the coming pages, you'll encounter some of these stories.

This book is about women so angry at slavery and lynching that they risked their lives and reputations and pioneered new forms of public expression, including speeches in front of mixed-gender and mixed-race audiences that were considered scandalous and dangerous at the time. It's about women so furious at their lack of a franchise—the right to vote—that they walked 150 miles from New York City to Albany to petition for the vote, went on hunger strikes, and picketed outside the White House. Women so livid that they stayed angry for the decades—their lifetimes—it took to get the right to vote, first via the Nineteenth Amendment to the US Constitution, which was ratified in 1920, and then the Voting Rights Act of 1965, which ensured that citizens of all races had the right to vote. Their rage led them to acts of civil disobedience—marches and sit-ins and voting when it was not legal to do so—for which they were threatened, jailed, and sometimes beaten. Women who took conversations that had historically been whispered and chose instead to broadcast them via open-air rallies and in the pages of newspapers and in lawsuits before courts and juries and judges and in front of political conventions and committees in Congress.

Anger has often been the spark for long-lasting, legal, or institutional reform in the United States. In fact, most of us have been taught, as part of our patriotic American story, about how the founding fathers were driven by anger at injustice to break away from England during the American Revolution. Yet somehow rage has rarely been acknowledged as righteous and patriotic when it has originated with women, though women have often taken pains to mimic or reference the language and sentiments of America's founding while making their own angry demands for liberty, independence, and equality. So this book includes the story of an enslaved woman who demanded her freedom after hearing the stirring words of the Declaration of Independence. It includes the story of girls who toiled in dangerous, filthy factories and angrily walked off the job inspired by the ideas of America's founders to proclaim that they deserved fair pay and better working conditions. Yet despite the fact that these quests for freedom and fairness were directly inspired by the revolutionary language we have been taught to admire, these women's stories—unlike that of the founding fathers and their furious dumping of tea into Boston Harbor—have not been passed along to us as righteous or nation-shaping.

This book also aims to show how this anger—so instrumental to the nation's growth and progress—has never been celebrated, rarely even been noted in mainstream culture; how women are not praised for their fury and too often have had their righteous passions simply erased from the record. We are told about Rosa Parks as the reserved, elegant woman whose refusal to give up her seat kicked off the Montgomery Bus Boycott that in 1955 would set ablaze the civil rights movement. But we are not taught that Parks was also a fervent activist with the civil rights organization the NAACP, investigating rape claims in the Jim Crow South, where discrimination and segregation were the law. We are never forced to consider that rage—and not just patience, sadness, or strength—was behind the actions of the few women's heroes we're ever taught about in school, from Harriet Tubman, who escaped slavery and went on rescue missions to free scores more enslaved people, to Susan B. Anthony, a lead agitator for gaining women the right to vote, who died before she ever got the chance to cast a ballot legally. Instead, we are regularly fed cultural messages that suggest that women's rage is at best a footnote and at worst irrational, dangerous, or laughable.

This book is about how anger has worked for men in ways that it has not for women, how men can wage yelling campaigns and be credited with understanding—and compellingly channeling—the passion felt by their supporters, while their female opponents can be booed and mocked as shrill or screechy for speaking too loudly or forcefully into a microphone. This is about women, some of whom have been angry for a long time but didn't have an outlet for it, didn't realize how many of their neighbors, their coworkers, their friends and mothers and sisters felt the same until someone yelled, loud and fierce, and everyone heard her. It's about women—maybe even your mothers, aunts, grandmothers—who found themselves holding signs at the Women's March in January 2017 and experienced a kind of awakening there, and wondered for the first time how on earth they'd been lulled to sleep in the first place. (One-third of those women had never been to a political protest before.)

Which means that this is also a story about women's anger at one another: at the kinds of privileges and incentives certain women, often white or wealthy, have been offered in exchange for shutting off or turning down their anger, and about the price other women—

nonwhite and especially Black women—have paid, always having *had* reasons to be angry and having rarely been offered relief or reward for the act of suppressing it.

This is a book that seeks to identify the warmth and righteousness of women's rage, but not simply to cheer it. Because it does have limits and dangers; of course anger can do harm. Anger at injustice and inequality is in many ways exactly like fuel. It can drive—on some level *must* drive—noble and difficult crusades. But it is also combustible, explosive; its power can be unpredictable and can burn.

Here it's important to note that while often in this country we like to tell ourselves flattering stories about our history, much of what you will read in the volume ahead (and even some of what's already happened in this introduction!) is difficult, sometimes violent, and troubling. The United States is a country that was founded on land stolen from its original inhabitants; it became a nation via violent overthrow, built its economic power in large part on the enslavement of human beings, denied the majority of its citizens a right to vote over centuries. The long battles to address these injustices have often been brutally difficult, and sometimes deadly, for the people who fought them, and this book will contain tough language and descriptions of events that were cruel and are sometimes hard to read about. A cleaner, neater story wouldn't be a fully honest one, but please prepare for some material that might distress or alarm you.

As we survey snapshots of the history of women's political anger, what becomes obvious is the ebb and flow of its uses and reach, how anger births progress, which in turn often triggers a backlash so fierce it in turn provokes new reasons for rage, though they may only find their expression decades later. The first part of this book describes the low status of women in precolonial American society and how their anger over centuries of deep inequality spurred them to push for the right to vote, to abolish slavery, and to improve the conditions and wages of working people. Part Two is broken up into eight short chapters and focuses on political battles waged by women after they (or at least some of them) finally gained the right to vote in 1920, including struggles for civil rights, abortion rights, protections for the LGBTQ+ community, and more. Part Three tells the story of what happened after the 2016 election, when a woman for the first time achieved enough political power to win the nomination of a major political party to compete for the presidency but lost the election to a proud chauvinist, a moment that unleashed a new epoch of women's political anger, which in turn provoked a furious backlash, resulting in the 2024 defeat of another female candidate for the presidency by the same chauvinist. Because the impact of that 2016 election continues to shape our present political reality, I slow down and stretch out this part of the story. A lot changed after 2016 and continues changing right now, and I hope this book helps you find your way into and through this intense and sometimes scary period in our country's history.

In our era of renewed rage—and punishment for having expressed it!—this is a volume that examines how this emotion has functioned in our past, what it has brought us, and what damage it has done, at the same time that it questions where it will take this nation next. On some real level, it is bananas that women's rage has never been given its proper due, its historical credit, that too few historians and journalists have noticed the catalytic role, the spark, that furious women—

speaking alone or working together against tyranny or oppression or injustice—have played in shaping and reshaping this country, in moving it closer to where it must be if it is to fulfill its patriotic, and yet unmet, promise of equality. This book is a start: exploring how women's and girls' anger has brought us to where we are today and, I hope, fortifying your impulse to use your anger to lead us now and in the future.

PART ONE
Colonial Period–1920

• *1* •

Containment of Women

For centuries, women have been treated in law and custom as inferior to men, the very men who wrote those laws and enforced those social customs. This would logically make anyone mad. But the furious female is—we are told to this day in countless ways, both subtle and stark—unnatural. She is ugly, emotional, out of control, sick, unhappy, unpleasant to be around, unpersuasive, irrational, crazy, childish. Above all, she must not be heard.

The brank—also known as a scold's bridle or a witch's bridle—was a sixteenth-century European torture device used to muzzle a defiant or cranky woman, her head and jaw clamped into a metal cage. Some of the bridles, which were made of iron, included tongue depressors that would be inserted into the woman's mouth; some of those had spikes on the bottom to pierce the tongues of unruly women should they insist on speaking out of turn. The Tower of London features an internally spiked metal neck collar dating from 1588, labeled a "collar for torture," but described in guidebooks as a device to be "put around the necks of scolding or wayward wives."

Despite attempts to physically or otherwise shut them up, angry women have been waging their battle for independence and equality, against politicians, preachers, and the popular press, since well before America's founding. But some of the earliest, most formative battles were on a smaller, closer scale: at home, pushing back against the institution of marriage. Why? Because women's oppression was not limited to the public sphere, where they were denied the rights of citizenship—like voting rights—and equal opportunity to work or own property or get an education. Women's oppression started in, and all those other facets of it were enabled by, one of the smallest units of society: the family.

There was no way to imagine women's social and political independence if they were not fully free even in their own homes. Marriage laws in colonial America were highly restrictive contracts, which some crusading married women fought to change. There were also women who chose to live singly. These unmarried women were considered pitiable or abnormal, but they were partly responsible for the social and economic upheavals that have made the possibility of independent life for today's women so much more plausible.

In the early colonial United States, the family was the center of social control. In Plymouth, in the Massachusetts Bay Colony, and in New Haven, in Connecticut, during the seventeenth century, unmarried people were required to live with families that were "well governed" by a churchgoing, land-owning man. Unmarried women were expected to stay home and serve the families with whom they lived and never enter the world in a way that might convey independence.

Keeping women dependent on men—their husbands and fathers and brothers, the kinds of people who at the time could hold jobs, earn money, and own land—was a way of keeping them powerless. Permitting them land gave them some degree of economic autonomy, and even opened up the possibility that they could demand a vote in the communities in which they owned land, so the practice was quickly discouraged.

For example, the town fathers of Salem, Massachusetts, very briefly allowed unmarried women their own property, until the governor amended the oversight by noting that in the future it would be best to avoid "all presedents & evil events of graunting lotts unto single maidens not disposed of." Because, as historian Alice Kessler-Harris has observed, the possibility of land ownership created a path to existence outside marriage, other colonies "began to recognize that giving land to women undermined their dependent role" and thus took measures to limit the option. In 1634, a bill was introduced to the House of Delegates in Maryland proposing that land owned by a spinster must be forfeited should she fail to marry within seven years. This was just part of how women who were not married, for one reason or another, were shamed socially and punished through policy. The term "spinster" was derived from the word "spinner," which, since the thirteenth century in Europe, had been used to refer to women, often widows and orphans, who spun cotton, wool, and silk into thread for fabric. By the sixteenth century, spinster referred to unmarried women, many of whom made themselves valuable in households by taking on the ceaseless, thankless work of textile manufacture into old age. In the New World, "spinster" gained a more precise meaning: In colonial times, it indicated an unmarried woman over the age of twenty-three and under the age of twenty-six. At twenty-six, women without spouses became "thornbacks," a reference to a sea-skate with sharp spines covering its back and tail. It was not a compliment.

Boston bookseller John Dunton wrote in 1686 that "an old (or Superannuated) Maid, in Boston, is thought such a curse as nothing can exceed it, and look'd on as a dismal spectacle." But in fact, the "dismal spectacle" of unmarried womanhood was quite rare in the colonies. Many more men than women were settlers, creating a high sex ratio, in which men outnumber women, a dynamic that usually results in high marriage rates and low marriage ages. As Benjamin Franklin noted in 1755: "Hence, marriages in America are more general, and more generally early, than in Europe."

Almost the only kind of woman who might assert individual power was the wealthy widow, afforded social standing since she had been married and was a legal inheritor of money or property, but left without a master. This was rare. Most widows were poor, with no means to support themselves or their children, and lived at the mercy of their communities for help in feeding and housing themselves and their families. Mostly, unmarried women were considered a drain on society and on the families with whom they were forced to find refuge.

The early American attitude toward marriage, and men's and women's roles within it, was influenced by the English policy known as coverture, in which a woman's legal, economic, and social identity was "covered" by the legal, economic, and social identity of the man she married; her identity as a separate person was wiped away the moment she said "I do." William Blackstone's *Commentaries on the Laws of*

England interpreted coverture as meaning that "the very being or legal existence of the woman is suspended during the marriage, or at least is incorporated and consolidated into that of the husband: under whose wing, protection, and cover, she performs every thing. . . . A man cannot grant any thing to his wife, or enter into covenant with her: for the grant would suppose her separate existence; and to covenant with her, would be only to covenant with himself."

"In its strictly economic aspect the traditional marriage contract resembled" the relationship "between master and servant," writes historian Nancy Cott. Coverture prevented wives from keeping their own wages, entering into contracts, or suing someone in court, what legal historian Ariela Dubler has called "a stunning array of status-defining legal restrictions." And while scholars have shown that many women in Europe and the New World found ways to act independently, both within their homes and in the outside world, the foundational unfairness of marriage laws made it a tough battle. For women who escaped marriage and coverture, there were other roadblocks to thriving. There were only a few poorly paid professions at which they could earn a meager wage; they might be midwives, seamstresses, caretakers, governesses, or tutors, all jobs that mirrored broader ideas about women's nature as nurturers.

The colonies' violent break from England, the American Revolution, on which the nation was officially founded, complicated gender relations. For one thing, it drained households of their able-bodied men, who fought the British in the 1770s, the 1780s, and in the War of 1812. These conflicts, followed by an era of exploration, which would draw men west and leave tens of thousands of women back east, scrambled sex ratios across the country, with disproportionately high numbers of women on the East Coast and disproportionately high numbers of men in the West.

But the rethinking of women's relationship to marriage wasn't just about numbers. The end of the eighteenth century was a time of political instability; the War of American Independence was followed by the French Revolution, which helped spawn the Saint-Domingue revolution that freed enslaved people and established the Republic of Haiti in 1804. Power structures were crumbling under the weight of ideas about liberty, personal freedom, and representation in this period known as the Enlightenment. In England, author Mary Wollstonecraft challenged the French philosopher Jean-Jacques Rousseau's vision of women as submissive to their husbands and instead pushed for female education and independence. She angrily declared war in 1792's *A Vindication of the Rights of Woman* on "the sensibility that led [Rousseau] to degrade woman by making her the slave of love."

Women were angry at the laws and customs that boxed them in. The language of freedom and equality that fired the Revolution "provided the women's rights movement with its earliest vocabulary," historian Mary Beth Norton argues. Lee Virginia Chambers-Schiller describes how "beginning in about 1780 women in the middle and upper classes . . . manifested a dramatic new form of female independence. In increasing numbers, the daughters of northeastern manufacturers, merchants, farmers, and 'poor professionals' rejected the 'tie that binds'": marriage.

All Men Would Be Tyrants

Married and single, women began to use revolutionary rhetoric to push for their own rights.

In the spring of 1776, Abigail Adams wrote a letter to her husband John in which she warned, "Do not put such unlimited power into the hands of the husbands." John would become America's first vice president and its second president, and in that 1776 note, Abigail cautioned him that women denied equal rights and opportunities would ultimately rise up, just as had the male colonists who birthed this nation over their ire at being taxed and policed without government representation. "Remember all men would be tyrants if they could," Abigail noted sharply. "If particular care and attention is not paid to the ladies, we are determined to foment a rebellion." Abigail was purposely using language that mirrored that of her husband's revolutionary rhetoric: In the period in which she was writing to him, the "tyrant" was King George of England, against whom the colonists were fomenting a "rebellion" that was a war that formed this nation. Her assertions extended beyond the domestic: They were pointed and political. And yet, in the founding documents of the new nation, the revolutionary white men had promptly codified into law precisely the kinds of inequalities that they had so furiously fought; they built their country out of a genocide of its native inhabitants, the enslavement of African Americans, the denial of the vote and full economic, legal, and social equality to women.

The notion of individual liberty during the revolutionary era was sharply at odds with the limitations put on some of America's inhabitants by marriage and by slavery. Marriage and slavery were not equivalent practices. Enslaved people were treated as chattel, counted in the Constitution as three-fifths human; they could be purchased and sold and had no freedom, no rights over their own bodies. Marriage, while a contract by which women lost rights and identities, was one that free people, acknowledged as human beings, officially entered into of their own choice (though any number of economic, family, or community pressures may have pushed them into choosing marriage). Through marriage, wives gained economic advantage, the rights of inheritance; they also enjoyed social and religious approval and an increase in status.

But the similarities between slave and marital law show how political, social, and sexual power over a population can be enforced by both urging marriage and by forbidding it, as well as how systems of racism and sexism doubly oppressed Black women. In the United States in the years before the Civil War, marriages between enslaved people were not legal, which both prevented the formation of legally sanctioned unions and allowed slavers to have sexual relations with people they enslaved without violating a marital bond. Conversely, some slave owners forced enslaved people into unwanted marriages, perhaps to produce more enslaved children or to cement family ties that might discourage escape. "[W]hen they could not marry whom they chose under circumstances of their own choosing, some enslaved people chose not to marry at all," historian Frances Smith-Foster writes, citing Harriet Jacobs, an enslaved woman who, prevented from marrying the free man she loved and told to choose a husband from among other men her owner enslaved, asked, "Don't you suppose, sir, that a slave can have some preference about marrying?"

Of course, enslaved women and men fell in love, married on their own terms, and created loving families all the time. But those families often were separated by sale; women and girls were forced to bear children by their owners and their owners' sons. Control over women's marital and reproductive lives was one of the surest ways to suppress their power.

And yet, despite tremendous risk, some enslaved women found ways to protest their treatment, and ultimately to free themselves and others using the very tools created by America's founders. Elizabeth Freeman, known then as Mum Bett, was born into slavery in upstate New York around 1744. When she was just seven years old, she was torn away from her parents and sent to serve in the household of their owner's daughter in Massachusetts, who was said to be particularly vicious and violent. The master of the house was less cruel, but Freeman understood that whether kind or abusive, no human should enslave another. "Any time while I was a slave, if one minute's freedom had been offered to me, and I had been told I must die at the end of that minute I would have taken it—just to stand one minute on God's earth a free woman—I would."

She grabbed her opportunity at freedom after she happened to hear a reading of the revolutionary rhetoric of the Declaration of Independence. In angry response to abuses she suffered at the hands of the people who enslaved her, including being hit with hot kitchen tools, she used the principles of the Declaration to petition for her freedom. The next day she went to the office of a local attorney, Theodore Sedgwick, and said, "I heard that paper read yesterday, that says, 'all men are born equal,' and that every man has the right to freedom. I am not a dumb critter; won't the law give me my freedom?" Sedgwick filed a lawsuit on Freeman's behalf, which she won. Her case was among those that would become the basis for the abolition of slavery in Massachusetts several years later. It was a demonstration of how outrage at injustice could in time spark the reform of law and policy.

• 2 •

Declaration of Sentiments

The mid-1800s were a time of growing political agitation and changed possibilities for American women. Improvements in infrastructure—better roads, canals, and the building of railroads—made it easier for women to leave rural homes and head to growing cities to work as seamstresses and hatmakers, governesses and laundresses. Many of the poorest, including free Black women in the North and South, worked in domestic service—as housekeepers, maids, cooks, and servants—for the growing class of urban industrialists who owned factories or mills or financed industry as bankers and investors. Poorly paid and overworked, these female laborers' behaviors were monitored by bosses, neighbors, clergy, and boardinghouse mistresses. But the concentration of them within cities, where they could encounter a wider variety of potential partners and friends and earn a little bit of money, meant that for the first time in the United States, single women were taking up space in economic, public spheres.

In these places, and in others, including the religious revivals of the period, which encouraged people to improve and morally uplift society, women were meeting one another outside the home. As the nation grew, the question of whether new territories would be slave or free was forcing a crisis. Women, encountering one another in schools and factories and religious contexts, were participating in that conversation and forming networks around a handful of social movements that would alter the future of the nation.

The social crusades of the nineteenth century included struggles against slavery; for women's right to vote; to protect workers, including children, from exploitation; and for temperance. The concerns behind these efforts were connected to one another. For example, many organizers for workers' rights understood that without the right to vote for elected officials, women workers could not create public policy to regulate businesses that harmed laborers. One of the fights that seems strangest to us today was the temperance movement, which eventually successfully outlawed the sale of alcohol, but it too had its roots in gender inequality: Women who fought for temperance did so in part out of a desire to protect wives and daughters abused by drunk husbands; it is, in fact, a reflection of the suffocating sexist limitations of that period that it seemed more practical and realistic to make drinking illegal at a federal level, than to alter the laws and customs that gave husbands power over their wives, and wives little remedy against violence and ill treatment within their marriages. Despite the very real limits on women's liberty, these movements were made possible by the changing nature of female engagement with the world and new ideas about identity and dependence, and by a growing impatience and anger among women.

Abolitionist thinking naturally overlapped women's rights advocacy. In 1835, a founder of the American Anti-Slavery Society, William

Lloyd Garrison, would publish a letter written by Angelina Grimké, the daughter of a Southern plantation owner, in his abolitionist newspaper, *The Liberator*. Grimké and her sister Sarah would go on to be leading abolitionists, sympathetic also to the fight for women's rights, and among the first women in America, along with Maria Stewart, to give speeches to "promiscuous" crowds—meaning mixed audiences of men and women. It was in the early 1830s that Stewart, the daughter of free Black parents from Connecticut, became the first American woman to address mixed-race audiences, and the first Black woman to give public lectures on both the abolition of slavery and women's rights. In 1837, Black and white American women came together for the first of three conferences on ending slavery. The second of those three conventions, held in Philadelphia, was seen as posing such a threat to the powerful that the hall in which it was to be held was burned to the ground. At the World Anti-Slavery Convention in London in 1840, women attendees—including Elizabeth Cady Stanton and Lucretia Mott—were barred from speaking, but many met one another for the first time, and, furious about being excluded, together started to put down the roots of the American movement for women's suffrage, the right to vote.

In 1848, two hundred women and forty-odd men met in Seneca Falls, New York, to draft the Declaration of Sentiments, a document modeled on the Declaration of Independence. The Declaration of Sentiments was also a statement of independence—noting that "all men *and women* are created equal." It was a direct attack on male power to keep women down and a seeming return on Abigail Adams's promise of rebellion: "The history of mankind is a history of repeated injuries and usurpations on the part of man toward woman," the

Declaration read in part, claiming that the purpose of taking away women's control over their own lives had been "the establishment of an absolute tyranny over her."

And then they described that tyranny:

> He has never permitted her to exercise her inalienable right to the elective franchise. [In other words, he has forbidden her from voting . . .]
>
> He has compelled her to submit to laws, in the formation of which she had no voice . . . [. . . and has controlled her with laws she had no opportunity to shape.]
>
> He has made her, if married, in the eye of the law, civilly dead. [In other words, a wife has no individual rights . . .]
>
> He has taken from her all right in property, even to the wages she earns. [. . . and he takes ownership over everything that belongs to her.]
>
> . . . In the covenant of marriage, she is compelled to promise obedience to her husband, he becoming, to all intents and purposes, her master—the law giving him power to deprive her of her liberty, and to administer chastisement . . . [In other words, a wife is essentially the slave of her husband . . .]
>
> He has so framed the laws of divorce . . . as to be wholly regardless of the happiness of women—the law, in all cases, going upon the false supposition of the supremacy of man, and giving all power into his hands. [. . . who has all the power in the relationship, legally.]

> He has monopolized nearly all the profitable employments, and from those she is permitted to follow, she receives but a scanty remuneration. [In other words, women's opportunities to work for pay are very limited . . .]
>
> He closes against her all the avenues to wealth and distinction, which he considers most honorable to himself. As a teacher of theology, medicine, or law, she is not known. [. . . by men who do not allow women to work in profitable or noble fields . . .]
>
> He has denied her the facilities for obtaining a thorough education—all colleges being closed against her. [. . . or even to learn and advance through a college education.]
>
> He allows her in Church as well as State, but a subordinate position . . . [In other words, no matter where she goes, she is treated as less than . . .]
>
> He has endeavored, in every way that he could to destroy her confidence in her own powers, to lessen her self-respect, and to make her willing to lead a dependent and abject life. [. . . and he makes sure she knows it.]

It was a deeply rebellious document. By making it a play on the Declaration of Independence, the suffragists were using the language and logic of righteous rage that America admired—the rage of the founders, white men who were furious about impositions on their liberty by the king—and using that blueprint to express anger on behalf of women whose freedoms had been limited by those very founders.

The women who wrote it knew that it wasn't going to be warmly received. "We anticipate no small amount of misconception, misrepresentation, and ridicule."

They predicted correctly. As the historian Marjorie Spruill has noted of the Seneca Falls meeting, "Outraged newspaper editors denounced the convention as shocking, unwomanly, monstrous, and unnatural, or ridiculed them as Amazons or love-starved spinsters." The *New York Herald* publisher James Gordon Bennett, Sr., a rabid opponent of both the abolition of slavery and suffrage for women, called the activists a "motley gathering of fanatical mongrels, of old grannies, male and female, of fugitive slaves and fugitive lunatics." He predicted that the activists' goals would lead to total societal breakdown: "Full consummation of their diabolical projects would reduce society to the most beastly and promiscuous confusion." More pathetically, one unsigned article in the *Daily Oneida Whig* of Utica, New York, wondered, "Was there ever such a dreadful revolt? This bolt is the most shocking and unnatural incident ever recorded in the history of womanity. If our ladies will insist on voting and legislating, where, gentlemen, will be our dinners?"

Repression and Convulsion

Sometimes the mere public expression of women's anger was its own innovation. "Men and angels give me patience," Elizabeth Cady Stanton wrote to Susan B. Anthony in 1852, frustrated by how the demands of motherhood and wifely duty stifled her ability to express her political anger through writing and speaking. "I am at the boiling point! If I do not find some day the use of my tongue on this question

I shall die of an intellectual repression, a woman's rights convulsion."

The speeches of female suffragists of the nineteenth century to audiences of mixed genders and races, starting with Maria Stewart and the Grimké sisters, provided a radical new model for women's participation in public, civic, and political life. Suffragists' open-air rallies and parades in support of the vote overturned expectations for female behavior and manners. Suffragists made practical inroads in other ways as well.

Many reformers were single, or at least excruciatingly aware of the gender limitations of the marriage model. When abolitionist and suffragist Lucy Stone married Henry Blackwell in 1855, the couple asked their minister to distribute a statement protesting marriage's inequities. It read, in part, "While acknowledging our mutual affection by publicly assuming the relationship of husband and wife . . . this act on our part implies no sanction of, nor promise of voluntary obedience to such of the present laws of marriage, as refuse to recognize the wife as an independent, rational being, while they confer upon the husband an injurious and unnatural superiority." Stone kept her last name, and generations of women who have done the same have been referred to as "Lucy Stoners."

The Polish-born Jewish suffragist and abolitionist Ernestine Rose, angry that her inheritance had been forfeited when she refused to marry the man her father had promised her to against her will, dedicated herself in part to a legal campaign to reform women's property laws in the United States. She lobbied through the 1850s alongside Elizabeth Cady Stanton and Susan B. Anthony for a set of reforms called married women's property acts, which would eventually pass in New York and be adopted by other states, and permit wives to keep more rights to inheritances and property than ever before.

Suffragists and abolitionists often battled alongside one another. Frederick Douglass, the great abolitionist leader who had escaped slavery, was one of the few men who attended the convention at Seneca Falls at which Stanton drafted the Declaration of Sentiments. Of Stanton, Douglass would later note that she considered the right to vote the most important: "She saw more clearly than most of us that the vital point to be made prominent, and the one that included all others, was the ballot, and she bravely said the word." Douglass would also later claim that "there are few facts in my humble history to which I look back with more satisfaction than to the fact . . . that I was sufficiently enlightened at that early day, and when only a few years from slavery, to support [her] resolution for woman suffrage."

It seemed there was a possibility that the young nation's majority, enslaved Black men and women along with all American women and especially those in the exploited working class on whose labor the country's economy and political power were being built, might come together, uniting around what they understood to be their linked conditions, ready to do battle against the white patriarchal minority power that oppressed them. The fight would be for abolition, for women's suffrage, and for reform of exploitative capitalism.

The Ballot Box Divide

But power, especially power held by a minority population, has ways of preserving itself against attack by an allied majority. After the Civil War ended in 1865 and enslaved people were officially freed, Americans were faced with the question of who should get the vote: The Fifteenth Amendment to the Constitution would give the right to vote to Black men, but not to women of any race. Some of those who were most committed to both abolition and women's suffrage sided with the granting of Black men the vote over women; Frederick Douglass, for example, believed Black men to be in greater need, due to the violent treatment they faced, and because white women already enjoyed some political power via their white husbands.

But other activists saw the move to grant citizenship and the vote to Black men as a way to strengthen systemic sexism by defining fully enfranchised citizenship for the first time as masculine. Nowhere in the Constitution had women been explicitly denied the right to vote until the passage of the Fifteenth Amendment. "The sons of pilgrims" in Congress, Stanton wrote, were simply "trying to get the irrepressible 'male citizen' into our immortal constitution." And the formerly enslaved abolitionist and suffragist Sojourner Truth is reported to have said, "There is a great stir about colored men getting their rights, but not a word about the colored women. And if colored men get their rights, and colored women not theirs, the colored men will be masters over the women, and it will be just as bad as it was before."

Some white suffragists, including Stanton and Susan B. Anthony, were livid at having put aside their emphasis on women's right to vote to focus on abolition through the Civil War. They were so angry at their abolitionist allies for what they interpreted as political abandonment that they struck out fiercely, revealing their own deep racism.

Stanton began giving speeches in which she spoke freely of her dislike for the Black men she was outraged would now be able to cast votes while white women like herself would not. After years of working toward women's suffrage and abolition, she wrote in 1865, "It becomes a serious question whether we [white women] had better stand aside and see 'Sambo' [a racial slur against Black Americans] walk into the kingdom first." Activist forces were further splintered by the strategic pitting of women's suffrage against Black male suffrage in various state contests.

Ignoring the pleas of her fellow suffragists, Susan B. Anthony accepted the offer of George Francis Train, a racist businessman who had opposed abolition, to fund a women's suffrage publication called *The Revolution*. Anthony and Stanton toured Kansas with Train, denouncing the Republican Party (which supported Black male suffrage) and standing by his side as he made, in the words of historian Andrea Moore Kerr, "pronouncements about the dangers of black suffrage."

Train was pitting the prospects of white women against those of Black American men by offering Anthony the support and economic resources she was desperate for but not getting from her former allies. As Anthony explained at the time about her association with Train: "All there is about him is that he has made it possible for us to establish a paper. If the Devil himself had come up and said ladies I will help you establish a paper I should have said 'Amen!'" In this paper, Anthony and Stanton pushed an ever more racist line of argument, Kerr writes, "making frequent references to the 'barbarism,' 'brute force,' and 'tyranny' of black men."

In 1869, during the months after the Fifteenth Amendment had been passed by Congress and activists were working to get it ratified by the states, there was an ugly showdown at the annual gathering of the American Equal Rights Association. Though Train had by then backed away from *The Revolution*, Anthony and Stanton were still agitating against ratification of the Fifteenth Amendment, while their fellow suffragist and staunch supporter of Black male suffrage, Lucy Stone, the woman who had insisted on keeping her own name after she married, was trying to herd the rest of the suffragist and abolitionist allies into line in support of the amendment—and of what she imagined might be a future *Sixteenth* Amendment that would bring women the vote as well.

"It is still true today over almost this entire country that no black man or woman finds the same sort of recognition either in public or in private that the white man or woman finds," Stone had said in a speech, as she worked desperately to soothe suspicions that all of the suffrage movement was opposed to African American men getting the vote. Stone correctly feared that if Stanton and Anthony's racist arguments against the Fifteenth Amendment worked to doom its ratification, it would be suffragists who'd be blamed. "It is not true that our movement is opposed to the Negro," Stone wrote anxiously to fellow suffragists. "But it will be very easy to make it so, to the mutual harm of both causes. . . . I feel dreadfully hurt by this new load we have to carry, and there is no need of it."

The Fifteenth Amendment was, finally, ratified. And the fantasized Sixteenth Amendment, which Stone hoped would grant women the franchise, would not come to be . . . at least not for another fifty years, until it was, in fact, the Nineteenth Amendment. The racial tensions that had divided the women's movement did not lessen, and suffragists would split into two separate organizations: one headed by Anthony and Stanton, another by Stone. Here was a case of anger between two oppressed groups, and then in turn between individuals within those groups, getting in the way of coalition and progress. The groups would not come together for another twenty years, and the split would delay the progress of the suffrage movement by decades.

• 3 •

The Bumpy Road to Suffrage

After the Civil War, women's participation in work outside the home began to expand and so too did the efforts of angry women to push for their rights—to vote, to exert control over their own reproduction and sexuality, to enact protections over their rights as workers. They used a variety of strategies to advance their goals and their messages, but the ability of women to work for wages was key to the fights for both gender and racial equality, because earning money is key to independence. "No genuine equality, no real freedom, no true manhood or womanhood can exist on any foundation save that of pecuniary independence," said Susan B. Anthony at the turn of the twentieth century.

For middle-class reformers in the years after the war, writes the historian Rachel Seidman, new ideas about how "women *should not* be dependent on men" began to take hold, while for working-class women, there was a new consciousness about how—with husbands, fathers, and brothers at war or out West—they "*could not*" be dependent on men. About three million men had left home to fight in the Civil War; more than six hundred thousand of them died, on the battlefields and of disease, many tended to by women who had joined the war effort on both sides by working as nurses. The experience of single life and widowhood became far more common for America's women, both during the war and in the years that followed. These women went to work in ever greater numbers, in many cases because they had to, but their wage-earning in turn awakened in them an awareness of and anger toward gender and class injustices.

A former teacher, Virginia Penny, wrote an 1869 book, *Think and Act*, about the challenges of income inequality facing working women who were increasingly living independent of men. She pushed for equal-pay protections from the government, and even suggested taxing better-paid single men to help support unmarried women. Around the same time, Aurora Phelps of the Boston Working Women's League petitioned for "Garden Homesteads," tracts of land near Boston to be given or paid for by the government to unmarried women willing to work them, an imagined East Coast equivalent to the land being given away by the government in the West as part of the Homestead Act, which encouraged white Americans to claim and develop land in the middle and western part of the country, pushing out and ultimately exterminating the Indigenous people who had lived in those regions for centuries. The Penny and Phelps proposals certainly weren't going anywhere. But even without the right to vote, women were beginning to enter policy debates about how to make room for them in the world.

While progress on women's suffrage nationwide was stalled, there were a few communities where women were gaining the right to vote: in the frontier west, where some women went to seek fortune themselves (gaining it, grimly enough, via claims to the land that was being ripped from native populations). Lee Virginia Chambers-Schiller reports that prior to 1900, around 10 percent of land claims in two Colorado counties were filed by unmarried women, some of whom—like South Dakota homesteader "Bachelor Bess" Corey—were interested in the land grab of the Homestead Act. When Oklahoma's Cherokee Strip was opened by the government to homesteaders in 1893, Laura Crews raced her horse seventeen miles in under an hour to claim the piece of land that she would tend herself for years before oil was discovered on the property. This small but nearly unprecedented opportunity for independent women to buy property and keep it wasn't simply a real estate issue; land ownership had been long linked to the right to vote. America's first voters were not just white men, but white men who owned property. And the first women to petition for the vote were women who had managed to acquire property.

Perhaps not coincidentally, many of the Western territories in which women staked out land were the very first places in which women's suffrage would eventually be established, some before passage of the Nineteenth Amendment that would grant women the right to vote nationwide. Women could vote in Wyoming, Utah, Washington, Montana, Colorado, Idaho, California, Arizona, Kansas, Oregon, Nevada, Oklahoma, South Dakota, Michigan, and Alaska before 1920, while women in the more urban, established Eastern states (save for New York) had to wait for the Constitution to change.

The revolutionary freedom of women seeking equal rights under the law provoked a new, more damning wave of misogyny, hatred of and prejudice against women, and the hard enforcement of laws keeping women in their place. In the presidential election of 1872, Susan B.

Anthony and fourteen other women were determined to vote. A few days before the election, Anthony angrily demanded to be registered to vote at her local polling site in Rochester, New York, righteously claiming that the Fourteenth Amendment to the Constitution established her as a citizen. She then showed up on Election Day to cast her ballot. Several weeks later, Anthony was arrested, jailed, and later fined one hundred dollars for breaking the law, though she refused to ever pay the fine.

In the late 1860s, Myra Bradwell petitioned for a law license and argued that the Fourteenth Amendment protected her right to practice law. The Illinois Supreme Court rejected her petition, ruling that because she was married, she had no legal right to operate on her own. When she challenged the ruling, Justice Joseph Bradley argued, "The paramount destiny and mission of women are to fulfill the noble and benign offices of wife and mother."

Meanwhile, the legal system was cracking down on anything that would help women escape or try to control those "benign offices." The Comstock Act of 1873, along with a series of state laws implemented soon after, made it illegal to distribute any materials deemed "obscene," including birth control and educational material about contraception to prevent pregnancies. States were outlawing abortion to end a pregnancy, which until then had been legal under some circumstances; by 1880, the procedure was mostly banned, except to save the life of the woman.

Monsters

The noisier women became demanding their rights, the more outrageous the patriarchy became in trying to stifle them. In this period, scientists around the world were working to justify the continued subjugation of women and nonwhite people by making medical claims about their supposed inferiority. German scientist Carl Vogt wrote in 1864, "The grown-up Negro partakes, as regards his intellectual faculties, of the nature of the child, the female, and the senile white." Gustave Le Bon, a prominent social psychologist, wrote in 1879 that "In the most intelligent races . . . there are a large number of women whose brains are closer in size to those of gorillas than to the most developed male brains. This inferiority is so obvious that no one can contest it for a moment; only its degree is worth discussion." Le Bon conceded that "Without a doubt there exist some distinguished women, very superior to the average man, but they are as exceptional as the birth of any monstrosity, as, for example, of a gorilla with two heads; consequently, we may neglect them entirely."

The American medical establishment built on European pronouncements to justify their recommendations to keep women's lives small, confined, and attached to men. In his 1873 *Sex in Education; or A Fair Chance for the Girls*, Harvard professor Edward Clarke argued that the female brain, if engaged in the same course of study as the male, would become overburdened and that wombs and ovaries would wither and die.

There was no doubt about a fear of rebellion that lay just beneath these diagnoses; this was a period in which more women were entering colleges and universities, and an educated woman posed a serious threat. As Le Bon wrote, "A desire to give [women] the same education . . . is a dangerous chimera . . . The day when, misunderstanding the inferior occupations which nature has given her, women leave the home and take part in our battles; on this day a social revolution will begin, and everything that maintains the sacred ties of the family will disappear." A chimera is not just an outcome that is desired but impossible, it is also a female monster in Greek mythology that breathes fire and has the head of a lion, the body of a goat, and the tail of a snake.

Independent women demanding equal rights were also often likened to another mythical Greek monster, Medusa, who was punished by the goddess Minerva, cursed with a head full of snakes and the ability to turn men into stone just by looking at them. Medusa was finally effectively disarmed when Perseus chopped off her head. Her story was not lost on the suffragist Susan B. Anthony, who observed in 1893 to the *Chicago Tribune* that women were asked to echo the sentiments of the men who ran the major newspapers, "and if they do not do that, their heads are cut off." In the same period, one preacher described the figure of the woman reformer, jostling into male spaces with her arguments for voting rights, as "a monstrosity of nature, a subverter of society . . . the head of Medusa, a bird of ill omen, a hideous specter, a travesty of all that is sacred and divine."

Yet for all this, women kept on getting angry, and they kept on bucking for change. And if the men in control would use fraudulent science to keep women down, women turned to their own creative strategies—from manipulation of traditionally feminized stereotypes, to calling on higher powers, mythological and otherwise—to lend credence to their efforts.

Higher Powers

Suffragists often used traditionally acceptable demonstrations of femininity, like sadness, to get their points across and disguise some of the rages that motivated them. In 1876, when five suffragists, including Susan B. Anthony, disrupted an official centennial celebration of the nation's one hundredth birthday, they handed out their own declaration of women's rights and read a speech about the injustice of women not having the vote, one that began by framing their political resistance as having been undertaken in grief, rather than fury: "While the Nation is buoyant with patriotism, and all hearts are attuned to praise, it is with sorrow we come to strike the one discordant note."

During the eighty-year suffrage battle, a concerted effort was made by feminists in the press to rehabilitate the image of legendarily prickly Susan B. Anthony as a kind of household goddess, despite the fact that she had chosen very intentionally not to marry or bear children and had shown nothing but scorn for the institution of marriage entered into by her colleagues, including Ida B. Wells, the groundbreaking Black journalist, whom she endlessly belittled for having wed. But just a few years before Anthony's 1906 death, as the movement to give women the right to vote ground on, *Pearson's Magazine* published a profile called "Susan B. Anthony at Home," in which the writer Ida Husted Harper marveled, "What a housekeeper is Susan B. Anthony, domestic in every fiber of her body!" Harper referred to the aged suffragist and labor leader as "Aunt Susan," and gushed about her skills at repairing worn clothes, "like a lovely grandmother . . . [she] never has suggested ways for repairing the damages of society with one-half the skill she employed in teaching her nieces her wonderful method of darning rents in garments and household linens." Historian Sara Hunter Graham writes that the process of taming Anthony's reputation by maternalizing her, making her seem like the mom she never was, "helped to replace the stereotypical image of a masculinized fanatic with a nonthreatening feminine heroine."

And damned if it didn't work. When Anthony died, the press reported warmly on mourners at her grave; the progressive labor organizer and politician Eugene V. Debs described her as "a moral heroine, an apostle of progress, a herald of the coming day." Graham argues that the remaking of Anthony's reputation meant that in this stage—the final haul—of the suffrage movement, "gone was the taint of extremism that suffragists believed had haunted the movement for decades; the parlor meeting had adopted 'Aunt Susan' as its patron saint, and suffragism had come of age."

When saintliness was not enough to move the needle, angry women had to invoke the gods directly. Take the eccentric case of Victoria Woodhull, the first woman ever to run for president of the United States in 1872. Woodhull was the first female Wall Street stockbroker, a self-proclaimed psychic, and an advocate for "free love," as opposed to oppressive marriages, as hers had been (she had divorced her alcoholic husband). Woodhull made outrageously bold assertions, once declaring, "We mean treason; we mean secession . . . We are plotting revolution; we will [overthrow] this bogus Republic and plant a government of righteousness in its stead." But she also believed herself to be a medium speaking on behalf of the long-dead Greek speechmaker Demosthenes, or channeling the Emperor Napoleon and his wife Josephine.

In this, Woodhull was not so different from some of her more officially respectable suffragist peers, some of whom took advantage of the period's fever for spiritualism to give a beyond-the-grave authority to their disruptive ideas. The table in Seneca Falls at which Elizabeth Cady Stanton would write the 1848 Declaration of Sentiments was one that had previously been used for séances to raise ghosts of the dead. And the nineteenth-century reformer and suffragist Frances Willard described how, in the midst of her travels on behalf of the temperance movement to outlaw alcohol, she sat down to pray one Sunday morning in 1876: "Upon my knees alone . . . there was borne in upon my mind, as I believe from loftier regions, the declaration: 'You are to speak for a woman's ballot as a weapon of protection to her home and tempted loved ones from the tyranny of drink.'"

In addition to getting God's go-ahead to push for voting rights as a means to curb the drinking of alcohol, as the historian Carolyn DeSwarte Gifford has noted, Willard "also received 'a complete line of argument and illustration' for her first speech on home protection, which she delivered later in the year at the Woman's Congress in Philadelphia." Indeed, Gifford writes, those women advocating for temperance via the vote—largely, it should be noted, as a means to protect women from physical abuse at the hands of drunken husbands—"had to be able to justify their political and suffrage activity religiously. It was absolutely essential for them to believe that their behavior sprang from an experience that convinced them that God wanted them, indeed called them, to vote."

Willard's more radical peer in the temperance movement, Carrie Nation, also cited God as working through her, not only to rage against the evils of alcohol, but also to physically destroy drinking establishments. As Nation would later recall, she was visited one day in 1900 "by a voice which seemed to me speaking in my heart, these words,

'GO TO KIOWA,' and my hands were lifted and thrown down." The interpretation of this message from the divine, Nation felt, "was very plain, it was this: 'take something in your hands and throw at these places in Kiowa [Kansas] and smash them.'" It was plainly God's direction, Nation maintained, that she gather up large rocks and use them to destroy saloons in Kansas, until her husband joked to her that she should use hatchets instead, which she described as "the most sensible thing you have said since I married you." (They divorced the next year.) Nation, who took the hatchet suggestion to heart and became famous for chopping up saloons all over the West, would go on to describe herself as "a bulldog running along at the feet of Jesus, barking at what He doesn't like."

Workers' Rights

The Progressive Era, from about 1890 to 1920, was a moment of enormous political and social upheaval, and much of it ran on rage. These decades included defining fights for fair labor practices and the rights of workers to join unions, public education, and a campaign against lynching, which in the South had become a deadly method of crushing the freedom and growing power of African Americans.

Immigrants from Europe were flooding East Coast cities, some moving toward the Midwest, while the Japanese population was growing on the West Coast. Chinese immigration had been halted by the racist Chinese Exclusion Act of 1882, but Chinese communities already in the country continued to expand. The American puzzle became more intricate; fights for unionization were linked to the suffrage campaign, which, in turn, influenced the push for the prohibition of alcohol and the struggle to establish new social welfare measures, like providing schooling for all kids. All these battles were tied to a stream of technological innovations that made new professions possible and employed new populations of Americans, in turn pulling them into the labor, suffrage, education, and civil rights struggles of the day.

Young women, many forced by financial crises in 1873 and 1893 to seek employment, arrived in cities looking for professional opportunities that were rapidly becoming more diverse. Stores for selling factory-made goods, alongside inventions such as the typewriter and telephone, created jobs for women as shopgirls, typists, telephone operators, and secretaries. In 1870, professional women accounted for less than 7 percent of the female workforce (not including farmworkers); that percentage would more than double by 1920.

Many women, especially poor immigrant women who labored in the factories that proliferated during this industrial era, worked long hours, seven days a week, in terrifying, unregulated firetraps. The deplorable conditions experienced by millions of female workers were at the roots of the labor struggle, which would be spurred forward in large part by women and girls. "The first industrial strikes in the United States [were] led and peopled by women," writes historian Nancy Cott, reporting on the account from a Boston newspaper of one of the first "turn-out" strikes in Lowell, Massachusetts, in the 1830s, in which "[o]ne of the leaders mounted a pump and made a flaming . . . speech on the rights of women." Young girls laboring at the Lowell Mills were inspired by the impulse that drove American revolutionaries. They spoke of their desire for better conditions, for freedom from oppression, in the same terms, declaring that "as our fathers resisted unto blood the lordly avarice of the British ministry, so we, their daughters, never will wear the yoke which has been prepared for us." They staged walkouts from the mills that helped kick off the American labor movement through which American workers formed unions to push for better pay and safer workplaces.

Once again, angry women wore the cloak of motherhood to lend credibility to their demands. Mary Harris Jones was a dressmaker and a teacher who became a labor organizer and an early member of the Industrial Workers of the World after her family died of yellow fever and her dress shop burned in the Great Chicago Fire of 1871. Jones opposed women's suffrage, believing it was a diversion of the upper classes, and argued that "you don't need the vote to raise hell." She herself raised a lot of hell and is responsible for the labor movement's famous call to action, "Pray for the dead and fight like hell for the living"; she also dressed in the clothes of an old woman, referred to the miners and other workers on whose behalf she fiercely battled as "her boys," and in her fifties became known as Mother. A US senator once condemned Mother Jones as the "grandmother of all agitators," to which she replied, "I hope to live long enough to be the great-grandmother of all agitators."

Twenty-five years her junior was Ella Reeve Bloor, a trade union organizer and socialist agitator who was a founding member of the American Communist Labor Party. Bloor helped the writer Upton Sinclair gather data for his exploration of urban poverty, *The Jungle*; she was a great supporter of women's rights and suffrage; she helped organize farm workers in Iowa in the 1930s—including an action in which dairy farmers protested low wages by dumping milk off delivery trucks. She was arrested thirty-six times and dubbed by *Life* magazine "the grand old woman of the U.S. Communist Party." And she was known as Mother Bloor. The historian Mary Triece has described both Mothers Jones and Bloor, while different in their particular politics, as having "enacted a persona of militant motherhood that proved successful in organizing entire families in struggles against corrupt bosses and company-owned towns across the country."

Beyond holding the banner of motherhood, some women agitators saw themselves as sisters within the labor movement. Clara Lemlich and her family fled her home country of Ukraine when she was seventeen after a pogrom in a nearby town, where the Jewish community was attacked and scores killed. Like many immigrants flooding into the US at the time, Lemlich took whatever work she could get to survive, including as a low-paid worker in a factory that manufactured shirtwaists, a style of women's shirt popular at the time; the conditions were awful. She worked, she would later write, from "sunrise to sunset seven days a week. Saturday till 4:30 o'clock. The shops were located in old dilapidated buildings, in the back of stores," and her shop had no heating or electricity. Lemlich became an outspoken organizer of workers demanding better treatment, safer conditions and higher pay. She faced arrests by police and endured multiple beatings—the police even broke her ribs—but she refused to stop.

On November 22, 1909, a big labor union meeting was called at Cooper Union, a university hall in lower Manhattan. For hours, the men on the stage spoke to the packed room about the working conditions, the police brutality, the horrors everyone there knew all too well. "But no [one] gave or made any practical or valid solution,"

Lemlich later wrote. The twenty-three-year-old labor organizer had had enough. "I wanted to say a few words," she called out, interrupting a speaker. An article from 1909 describes what happened next: "Willing hands lifted the frail little girl with flashing black eyes to the stage, and she said simply: 'I have listened to all the speakers. I would not have further patience for talk, as I am one of those who feels and suffers from the things pictured. I move that we go on a general strike!'" The next day, twenty thousand men and women laborers went out on strike, igniting a labor action that lasted for weeks and sparked further strikes—and improved labor conditions—over the coming years.

Two years later, on March 25, 1911, a fire at the Triangle Shirtwaist Factory, one of the few shirtwaist shops that had not agreed to strikers' demands, killed 146 workers, almost all of them women, the majority young immigrants. Its owners had locked the working girls inside to prevent theft, and the factory had no sprinkler system, one shoddy water hose, and a single rickety fire escape.

A week after the fire, Rose Schneiderman, a twenty-eight-year-old labor organizer who encouraged working women to form unions that would protect and defend their rights as workers, and who had witnessed some of the Triangle women leaping from the blaze to their deaths on a Greenwich Village street, stood at a memorial service for the dead at the Metropolitan Opera House and furiously admonished the well-heeled audience of mourners:

"I would be a traitor to these poor burned bodies if I came here to talk good fellowship. We have tried you good people of the public and we have found you wanting. . . . This is not the first time girls have been burned alive in the city. Every week I must learn of the untimely death of one of my sister workers. Every year thousands of us are maimed. The life of men and women is so cheap and property is so sacred . . . But every time the workers come out in the only way they know, to protest against conditions which are unbearable, the strong hand of the law is allowed to press down heavily upon us. Public officials have only words of warning to us—warning that we must be intensely peaceable . . . I can't talk fellowship to you who are gathered here. Too much blood has been spilled. I know from my experience it is up to the working people to save themselves. The only way they can save themselves is by a strong working-class movement."

Another of Schneiderman's speeches in 1911, in which she implored, "The worker must have bread, but she must have roses, too" became the mantra of the 1912 Bread and Roses Strike of female textile workers in Lawrence, Massachusetts, and an anthem in the labor and women's movements that were to come. Elizabeth Gurley Flynn, a radical socialist who married at seventeen but separated from her husband two years later, organized mining and textile strikes around the country, was arrested multiple times, and was memorialized in a popular song called "The Rebel Girl."

While factory unionizers often focused on the physical dangers in workplaces, the labor movement in education concerned itself primarily with fair pay, but was no less contentious in its argumentative style or aggressive actions. Margaret Haley, known in the press as the "Lady Labor Slugger," led the Chicago Teachers' Federation, one of the more militant teaching unions in the nation. She questioned assumptions that female teachers could be paid less after a 1910 National Education Association survey found that they were often the main earners of their families' income.

Haley understood that since women couldn't vote, teachers needed to align with the male labor movement, and decided to join her 97 percent female union to the blue-collar Chicago Federation of Labor, remaking teacher unionism as an urban political force and getting herself called by a conservative, anti-labor businessman, a "nasty, unladylike woman."

Full Steam Ahead

During these same years, other reformers—many of them suffragists, socialists, and labor agitators—were building the settlement house movement, creating residential spaces where rich and poor might come together to better understand and address class and racial injustice. Chicago's Hull House, founded by two activists, Jane Addams and Ellen Gates Starr, provided everything from childcare to continuing education.

Settlement houses were, in many cases, designed as places where single and divorced women might find community and a respectable life structure outside marriage; they were also a breeding ground for progressive economic policy that called for laws ensuring that workers earned fair wages and that the wealthiest paid their share of taxes. Frances Perkins, who like Schneiderman was a witness to the Triangle Shirtwaist fire and would work alongside her to push through workplace safety reforms, also worked at Hull House. Perkins would go on to become Franklin Delano Roosevelt's secretary of labor, the first woman appointed to a presidential cabinet, and the creator of Social Security, the government program that provides an income for older Americans. Florence Kelley, a suffragist, socialist, civil rights leader, and labor organizer who opposed child labor and sweatshops, fought for minimum wage laws and petitioned the Illinois legislature for eight-hour workdays for women and children; after leaving her husband, she moved to Hull House and then to the Henry Street Settlement, founded by social activist Lillian Wald, in New York.

The labor movement and the settlement house movement merged with the ongoing suffrage fight in natural ways. As Clara Lemlich explained, "The manufacturer has a vote; the bosses have votes; the foremen have votes; the inspectors have votes. The working girl has no vote."

An older generation of activists, including Susan B. Anthony and antilynching crusader Ida B. Wells, teamed with younger women who also picked up strategies from England's radical feminists. In the early twentieth century, young suffragist reformers Alice Paul and Lucy Burns studied new modes of resistance abroad with militant British reformers and returned to the United States prepared with new tactics, including hunger striking, chaining themselves to the White House fence, and burning President Woodrow Wilson's speeches. In 1912, twenty-five women hiked 150 miles from New York City to Albany to draw attention to the suffragist struggle, handing out leaflets and living on sandwiches, peanuts, and chocolate. In later years, Paul would draft the Equal Rights Amendment, a constitutional amendment that would have guaranteed equal rights regardless of gender. It read, simply, "Men and women shall have equal rights throughout the United States and every place subject to its jurisdiction;" it would be introduced in every congressional session from 1923 until 1972, when it finally passed but was not ratified by the states. (It has been reintroduced, though never passed, in every session since 1982; a recent push to ratify it has secured thirty-eight states, and in his final days in office, President Joe Biden declared it law, though scholars disagree about how binding that declaration is, and the second Trump administration will not recognize it as a constitutional amendment).

The racism that had divided the women's movement had by no means disappeared, nor would it anytime soon. In 1895 Susan B. Anthony had asked Frederick Douglass not to appear at a suffrage convention in the South, because she was trying to strategically win white women to the cause. And for all her youthful ideas and forward-looking energy, Alice Paul tried unsuccessfully to force her elder, Ida B. Wells, not to walk with her state's delegation in the enormous 1913 suffrage march on Washington, DC, and instead to march with the rest of the Black women suffragists where they'd been told to position themselves: behind all the white women. (Wells refused and marched with the rest of the Illinois marchers.) Neither did women of any race have the vote, nearly six decades after the first meetings of the Black and white women joining to push for abolition, and more than forty years after Douglass had joined Stanton at Seneca Falls.

On the day that Frederick Douglass died in 1895, he had spent the morning with Susan B. Anthony at a meeting of suffragists. In fact, he'd had such a good time that he had been in the midst of telling his wife about the meeting when he'd fallen to his knees, hands clasped, and his wife had simply believed that his pose was one of storytelling enthusiasm, not realizing that he was in fact dying.

"It is a singular fact," the *New York Times* reported in Douglass's obituary, "that the very last hours of his life were given in attention to one of the principles to which he has devoted his energies since his escape from slavery. . . . Mr. Douglass was a regularly enrolled member of the National Woman Suffrage Association, and had always attended its conventions." The obituary noted that his companion at the suffrage meeting that day was "Miss Anthony, his lifelong friend," and that when "Miss Susan B. Anthony heard of Mr. Douglass's death, at the evening session of the council, she was very much affected. Miss Anthony has a wonderful control over her feelings, but tonight, she could not conceal her emotion."

Frederick Douglass was seventy-eight at his death; Susan B. Anthony would die eleven years later at eighty-six. Elizabeth Cady Stanton, who had turned to such baldly racist language in her anger when Black men got the vote before women, was seventy-nine at the time of Douglass's death and would live another seven years. Near the end of his life, Douglass observed of their linked battles, "We should all see the folly and madness of attempting to accomplish with a part what could only be done with the united strength of the whole."

None of the three, of course, would live to see the passage and ratification of the Nineteenth Amendment, which would change the gender politics of the country forever. In 1919, Congress passed the Nineteenth Amendment; it was ratified by the states in 1920. For the first time in America's history, its female citizens could legally vote. Except that even then, it was not quite so clear or neat a victory.

White men have had a nearly exclusive grip on political, economic, social, and sexual power in the United States from its founding, despite being only around a third of its population. The way that a minority power protects itself from the potential uprising of a majority is to discourage unification of that majority. And the best way to discourage unification is to split the majority against itself by offering benefits and protections of power to some, while denying them to others. Clara Lemlich saw this in action in 1909 when she tried to unify girls and women in the garment factories of New York for better pay and working conditions. As historian Annelise Orleck documented, "Clara Lemlich complained that one strike she had been organizing was foiled when management 'told the Italian girls that the Jewish girls were striking because they hated Italians and didn't want to work with them. That was not true.'"

The Nineteenth Amendment—widely understood as the moment when "American women" got the right to vote—represented forward motion principally for white women, since Black people in the South were by 1920 prevented from voting by poll taxes, literacy tests, and the threat of lynching—the discriminatory Jim Crow laws that had arisen as a backlash response to emancipation from slavery and the Reconstruction years following the Civil War in which Black men had been elected to office and begun to gain greater economic and social power. Jim Crow laws would only be overturned by the civil rights laws of the mid-1960s.

And yet, over a century in which women had exercised increasing independence in the world, the movements that angry women had helped power had resulted in the passage of the Fourteenth, Fifteenth,

Eighteenth, and Nineteenth Amendments to the Constitution, changes to the law that redistributed power out of the hands of the white male minority and spread it more equally to the whole population.

Angry women had reshaped the nation.

PART TWO
1920–2016

• 4 •

The New Women— Backlash and Redirection

The (even partially realized) victory of women's suffrage seemed to send widespread women's political anger underground for several decades. As women's rights and liberties expanded legally, as the culture appeared to open up to new forms of equality and freedom, as women's lives became less restricted by homebound domesticity, a societal backlash arose to yank women backward, away from financial independence and reproductive autonomy.

The twentieth century dawned on a cultural landscape that was as remade as the political one.

Electric streetlamps had come to cities around the country, creating "white ways" with bright lights that made it feel safer for women to be on the streets at night. This development changed the kinds of jobs women could work, as well as the ways in which they could spend money and leisure time. Working-class young women in cities may have struggled economically, but the lit streets, nickelodeon theaters where viewers could watch movies for five cents, vaudeville houses showing live performances of song and dance, bowling alleys, music and dance halls that began to pop up everywhere meant that these women (and men), according to Kathy Peiss, "spent much of their leisure apart from their families and enjoyed greater social freedom than their parents or married siblings, especially married women." Young women "[p]utting on finery, promenading the streets, and staying late at amusement resorts became an important cultural style for many working women."

Peiss writes of the drive of some working-class women toward increased social freedoms, noting that single working women "were among those who flocked to the streets in pursuit of pleasure and amusement, using public spaces for flamboyant assertion." Although these so-called rowdy girls were criticized for immorality, Peiss writes, "young women continued to seek the streets to search for men, have a good time, and display their clothes and style in a public arena."

African Americans continued the great migration that had begun with the end of the Civil War from the South into Northern cities, while new waves of immigrants from Eastern Europe continued moving to New York City and other big urban centers. Black people and immigrants began to mix in urban centers, not always peaceably. But the coming together of different kinds of people helped the sharp class and ethnic lines begin to blur, if only slightly, producing new, liberated fashions in dress and entertainments.

Syncopated rhythms, originating in the Black neighborhoods of New Orleans, led to ragtime-era dance crazes, which in turn gave way to dance fads like the Charleston and the Black Bottom that would take hold in the Jazz Age. Working women of New York's Bowery and West Village neighborhoods began to experiment with cropped hair and shorter hemlines on dresses and skirts that made it easier and safer for them to work in factories—their long locks and full skirts used to get caught up in factory equipment, causing injuries. As these women became more visible on sidewalks and in public gathering places, middle- and upper-class women began to mimic their styles. Women were soon unburdening themselves of fashions that had, in the nineteenth century, weighed an estimated thirty pounds, turning to shorter skirts and looser fits.

In 1914, as courtship rituals moved away from family homes or closely watched community dance halls, the *Ladies' Home Journal* used the term "dating" in its modern sense. As centuries of sexual repression began to give way slightly, reformers took up the fight to make contraception more accessible. The fight to exert control over reproduction drew the attention of anarchist activists including the Russian-born Emma Goldman. Married twice herself, Goldman was an early proponent of gay rights; she was also a vocal, angry critic of marriage, which she felt condemned women "to life-long dependency, to parasitism, to complete uselessness, individual as well as social." As a nurse and midwife on the Lower East Side in the 1890s, Goldman had waged war on the Comstock Laws that barred the distribution of information about contraception and abortion. By the early twentieth century, she was smuggling birth control into the United States from Europe. She was also mentoring a young nurse and free spirit, Margaret Sanger.

Sanger, a married mother whose own mother had been pregnant eighteen times in twenty-two years and had died early of cervical cancer and tuberculosis, began writing pieces about sexual education for the socialist magazine *New York Call* in 1912. The next year she began work at the Henry Street Settlement and soon separated from her husband. In 1914 she published a newsletter called *The Woman Rebel*, which proclaimed that every woman should be "absolute mistress of her own body" and as such, should get contraception, which Sanger referred to as "birth control."

In 1916, Sanger opened a family planning clinic in Brownsville, Brooklyn; it was raided by police after ten days, and Sanger spent thirty days in prison. Five years later, the same year that Sanger and her husband finally divorced, she founded the American Birth Control League, which would later become the Birth Control Federation of America, and, in 1942, would be renamed the Planned Parenthood Federation of America, which continues today to offer women crucial reproductive health care; one in five women in the US has visited a center.

The new clothes that revealed more female flesh, the lightening of a limiting wardrobe, the push for more accessible means of preventing pregnancy, together they began to send a popular message. The press in the early twentieth century called the educated, wage-earning, socially liberated female "the new woman," and while she didn't always present as angry, her liberation from the cultural, political, and social binds of the past had been made possible by her foremothers' fury at those limitations. She wasn't popular with everyone.

"In our modern industrial civilization, there are many and grave dangers to counterbalance the splendors and the triumphs," President Theodore Roosevelt said at the beginning of a 1905 speech to the National Congress of Mothers. One of these dangers was the existence of women "who deliberately forego . . . the supreme blessing of children."

Roosevelt had become fretful after seeing the 1890 census of people living in America. The census showed fewer babies being born—a declining birth rate—and he began to worry about "race suicide," the idea that a white Anglo-Saxon failure to reproduce would damage the nation. Roosevelt, who supported many aspects of women's equality, including suffrage and women's involvement in labor, nonetheless blamed the declining fertility rate on those white women whose professional, political, and other nondomestic commitments were leading them to start families late and not at all. "A race is worthless," Roosevelt railed, "if women cease to breed freely."

After Roosevelt left the presidency in 1909, he continued to express his anxiety, clarifying that he was not worried about a lower birth rate for poor "pauper families with excessive numbers of ill-nourished and badly brought up children" but rather was concerned about the "voluntary sterility among married men and women of good life . . . If the best classes do not reproduce themselves the nation will of course go down."

Roosevelt's distinctions were rooted in the readily expressed racism of his time and in hostility toward Japanese and Chinese immigrants on the West Coast, whose higher birth rates seemed to threaten the whiteness of the nation. They were also an expression of judgment against the women exercising new forms of public freedom.

"The race, the race! Shouts the king, the president, the capitalist, the priest," wrote Emma Goldman in 1911. "The race must be preserved, though woman be degraded to a mere machine."

At the end of the nineteenth century, writes Chambers-Schiller, "the singlehood of women became a politically charged issue from which it was clearly understood that spinsterhood and independence were linked." This recognition, she continues, "inspired a political and cultural backlash which, in the 1920s, returned women to marriage and domesticity."

As women gained the right to go out, to earn wages, to live freer sexual and social lives, and to vote, men appeared ever more eager to tell them they'd better stay home and settle down.

Marriage Dislodged

In 1924, the *Yale Review* published an article by the sociologist William Sumner, who argued that the industrial age's new opportunities for women had "dislodged marriage from its supreme place in their interest and life plan. This is the greatest revolution in the conditions of the marriage institution . . . in all history . . . the importance of the fact that for great numbers of [women] it is no longer the sum of life to find husbands can easily be appreciated." The disruption of marriage as the single path for women—not to mention the impact that unmarried women, independently and in connection with one another as colleagues and activists, were having on politics, professions, and populations—was a threat that drew further cultural blowback.

The reverberations were sometimes hilariously obvious: Suffragists had often staged political "pageants" in which they wore sashes across their bodies emblazoned with VOTES FOR WOMEN. But 1921, the year following the ratification of the Nineteenth Amendment, brought a perversion of this display: the debut of the Miss America pageant, in which unmarried women showcased themselves solely as bodies to be judged for their physical attractiveness to men in competition against, as opposed to collaboration with, one another.

Women once again began to marry at younger ages. While the fertility rate would dip during the Great Depression of the early 1930s when the US economy tanked and many millions of Americans suffered through hunger, homelessness, and job loss, the 1930s would include a widespread backlash not just against the social liberties of the Jazz Age, but against the politics of independent female reformers of the progressive age.

These attacks were sometimes made, as they are today, by women who had come to see the regressive light from their own professional, political perches, with no acknowledgment of that hypocrisy. Journalist Rose Wilder Lane had worked outside the home throughout her adult life but wrote a *Ladies' Home Journal* article in 1936 called "Woman's Place Is in the Home." In it, she argued that feminist agitation had dangerously diminished the importance of the "deep-rooted, nourishing and fruitful man-and-woman relationship." A woman's real career, wrote Lane, the professional journalist, "is to make a good marriage."

Marry Early and Often

The back-to-back crises of the Depression and World War II, which America formally and fully entered in 1941 after Japan's attack on Pearl Harbor, drove many women, married and single, to get jobs. The iconic image of Rosie the Riveter, rolling up her blue coverall sleeves under the slogan "We Can Do It" helped inspire six million American women to join the workforce during World War II as men were shipped abroad to fight. For some white middle-class women who had never before had to work for wages, this was new. For the many Black women who had always worked, the opportunity for skilled jobs, albeit for less money than their white counterparts, expanded.

Once the war ended in 1945, women were nudged back to the kitchen. "'I want my wife waiting for me and I want my job waiting for me,'" one soldier in the South Pacific said, according to the historian Doris Kearns Goodwin in her chronicle of this period, *No Ordinary Time.* The War Department, major corporations, movies, magazines, and the mass media—all run by men—advanced that message despite the fact that the vast majority of women had enjoyed working outside the home. This was especially disorienting and concerning for women who needed to work to have enough money to pay the bills—often women of color and poor white and immigrant women. Following the war, women were laid off at an astonishing pace. One cartoon from the time captured the absurdity of the whiplash: a male manager is depicted firing a woman from her job and saying to her "so sorry, have suddenly remembered you are incapable of working in a factory."

The patriotic step back, as soon as soldiers returned from fighting in the war and the economy rebounded, was harsh and brought with it a whole new brand of enforced domesticity. Thanks to the GI Bill, a federal law that paid for college for returning soldiers, veterans were eligible for college educations that could propel them into the growing white middle class (white veterans were far more likely to be admitted to universities and thus have access to the education funds granted by the GI Bill).

The federal government also supported loans for people to buy homes in brand-new suburbs—many of which were restricted and barred Black residents—that would house the millions of children women were busy making, in what would become America's enormous baby boom. It was a neat system. Advertisers sold white women and men on an old, cult-of-domesticity-era ideal: that the highest female calling was the maintenance of a domestic sanctuary for men on whom they would depend economically. In order to care for the home, these women would rely on new products, like vacuum cleaners and washing machines, sales of which would in turn line the pockets of the husbands who ran the companies and worked in the factories that produced these goods.

The mid-twentieth-century push for white women was not simply to marry, but to marry early, before gaining a taste for independent life. A 1949 American Social Hygiene Association pamphlet advised that "Marriage is better late than never. But early marriage gives more opportunity for happy comradeship . . . for having and training children . . . promoting family life as a community asset, and observing one's grandchildren start their careers."

By the end of the 1950s, around 60 percent of female students were dropping out of college, either to marry or because the media blitz and realignment of expectations had led them to believe that further education would hurt their chances of finding a husband. College education, which had sped up women's freedom in the previous century, now worked, in part, to squash it. In his 1957 *Harper's* piece, "American Youth Goes Monogamous," Dr. Charles Cole, president of Amherst College, wrote that "a girl who gets as far as her junior year in college without having acquired a man is thought to be in grave danger of becoming an old maid." Cole sadly compared his female students, now in search of fiancés, to the women he'd taught in the 1920s, who he recalled attended college in hopes of launching a career, not finding a mate. In Barnard's graduating class of 1960, two-thirds of seniors were engaged before graduation and, as Gail Collins reports, at pre-graduation parties, engaged students were given corsages while singles were offered lemons.

In these years, around half of those brides were younger than twenty and fourteen million women were engaged by the time they were seventeen. Gloria Steinem, who would become a feminist leader and icon, was born in 1934, and recalled to me that, in her heavily Polish neighborhood in Toledo, Ohio, most women got married in high school. "I just didn't know that you could live without getting married, unless you were crazy," Steinem said of her youth, recalling a cousin who had never married, worked with the Red Cross in Europe, and had been regarded as mentally and emotionally unstable. "That was my image of the alternative," Steinem said. She remembered going to a Polish wedding reception at a bar where, "even though I was a very young teenager, I noticed that the bride was very depressed." Steinem finally approached and asked what was wrong, to which the sad bride replied, "You don't understand. I'm twenty." The expectation, Steinem explained, was that "you were supposed to get married at sixteen or seventeen and she'd been unable to find a proper husband. Now she was twenty, and they had married her off to some guy who was younger, which was terrible."

Women who were educated, thanks to the victories of a previous generation of activists, were sometimes left confused by the backward pressures of the society in which they lived. Author Judy Blume has described how, as a college student with ambitions to become a writer, she gave in to the expectation to marry young. Pregnant by the time she earned her degree, Blume recalled the disappointment she felt when she "hung [her] diploma over the washing machine." And as writer Nora Ephron explained in a 1996 commencement address at her alma mater, Wellesley College, about her own graduating class of 1962: "We weren't meant to have futures, we were meant to marry them. We weren't meant to have politics, or careers that mattered, or opinions or lives; we were meant to marry them. If you wanted to be an architect, you married an architect."

Whatever rage these women may have felt was buried deep within themselves as they upheld society's expectations of them to be compliant and serve the will of the men in their lives and keep home. These women were white; their husbands made a good living; they had nice homes and lawns, the latest appliances, fully stocked pantries. What on earth would they have to be angry about?

• 5 •

Walled Off

The domesticity of the 1950s has long been understood both as a reaction to the Great Depression and the World Wars, especially World War II, and the flooding into the working world of women in wartime. But it wasn't just about nudging women off factory floors and selling them blenders; it was also about forcing marriage back down the throats of women who had spent a century purging it as the central element of their identity. Or, rather, it was about forcing marriage back down the throats of some women, triggering different forms of resentment and hidden rage depending on race and class.

While marriage rates for middle-class white women soared through the 1940s and 1950s, for Black women, mid-twentieth-century conditions were very different. Since emancipation from slavery, African Americans had married earlier and more often than their white counterparts. In the years directly after World War II, thanks to the return of soldiers, Black marriage rates briefly increased further. However, as white women kept marrying in bigger numbers and at younger ages throughout the 1950s, Black marriage rates began to decrease, and the age of first marriage to climb. By 1970, there had been a sharp reversal: Black women were not marrying nearly as often or as early as white women.

It was not a coincidence. The expansion of the middle class was founded on the aggressive reassignment of white women to domestic roles within the idealized nuclear family—mom, dad, and two or three kids. At the same time, African Americans were excluded from the opportunities and communities that permitted those nuclear families to thrive. Put more plainly, the economic benefits extended to the white middle class, both during the 1930s and in the post–World War II years, did not extend to African Americans, and in fact sometimes came at the expense of Black flourishing.

Social Security, created in 1935 to support Americans of retirement age, did not apply to either domestic laborers, like maids and nannies, or farm workers, who tended to be African Americans, or Asian or Mexican immigrants. Discriminatory hiring practices, the low percentages of Black workers in the country's newly strengthened labor unions, and the reality that many colleges barred the admission of Black students also meant that returning Black soldiers had a far harder time taking advantage of the GI Bill's promise of a college education.

Then there was housing. The suburbs that bloomed around American cities after World War II were built for white families. William Levitt's four enormous Levittowns were suburban developments that grew and provided low-cost housing to qualified veterans with the backing of government agencies, the Veterans Administration and the Federal Housing Administration; the Levittowns had not one

Black resident. Between 1934 and 1962, the government subsidized $120 billion in new housing; 98 percent of it for white families.

Urban historian Thomas Sugrue reports that, in Philadelphia, between the end of the war in 1945 and 1953, "only 347 of 120,000 new homes built were open to blacks." As Sugrue writes, this inequality created a much higher demand for housing than was available to Black buyers, causing prices for homes open to Black families to rise wildly. African American residents were forced to live "crammed into old and run-down housing, mainly in dense central neighborhoods" that had been abandoned by white residents moving out to the suburbs. Banks routinely refused to offer home loans and mortgages to residents of minority neighborhoods, or offered loans at very high interest rates, suggesting that it was extremely risky to lend to African Americans.

The new freeways that threaded the suburbs to the urban centers where residents made their livings were often built by tearing down Black neighborhoods; those new roads regularly cut off Black residents from business districts and the public transportation that might connect them to jobs and public services. Postwar "urban renewal" projects supposedly intended to create public housing for poor Americans often involved the dismantling of nonwhite communities and the relocation of minorities to areas with few services.

These racist policies in Northern suburbs were a sneaky form of segregation. But in the South, outright segregation was the law, and while its supporters claimed that meant that Black and white people could have "separate but equal" opportunities and access to facilities like restaurants, pools, schools, buses, and theaters, in practice that promise was a lie. Schools for Black children were sorely underfunded, with furniture that was falling apart and few books. Black men and women were barred from many professions. These Jim Crow laws in the South also prevented Black men and women from voting. By establishing poll taxes—fines Black people had to pay to be eligible to vote—and trick tests—such as only allowing Black people to vote if they correctly answered impossible questions like guessing the number of beans in a jar—hundreds of thousands of Black voters were stripped of their voting rights.

When Black people were able to compete by gaining employment that might otherwise have gone to white people, buying houses near white neighborhoods, attempting to vote or enroll in white schools or interact with white women, the response, especially in the Jim Crow South, was often violent. It was an era of voter intimidation, lynching, cross burning, and property destruction by the racist and vicious white terror organization, the Ku Klux Klan.

These maneuvers cemented a cycle of economic disadvantage that made marriage—especially the kinds of traditionally patriarchal marriages that white women were being shooed into—less practical. If Black women were working all day (often scrubbing the homes of white women), it was impossible for them also to fulfill the at-home maternal ideal for which white women were being celebrated. If Black men had a harder time getting educations and jobs, earning competitive wages, or securing loans, it was harder for them to play the role of provider. If there were no government-financed suburban homes to fill with publicly educated children, then the nuclear family chute into which white women were being funneled was not open to most

Black women. There simply weren't the same incentives to marrying early or at all; there were fewer places to safely put down roots and fewer resources with which to nourish them.

It's not that Black women simply happened not to experience mid-1950s domesticity; they were actively excluded from it, trapped in another way: walled off in underserved neighborhoods by highways that shuttled fairly paid white husbands back to wives who themselves had been walled off in well-manicured, suffocating suburbs.

Burning with Rage

Not all women of the regressive, backward periods of the American mid twentieth century muted their rage, though some expressed their ire in the context of motherhood and marriage, which made it seem more reasonable.

In 1930, Fannie Peck was fed up with the limited professional opportunities available to the swelling population of African Americans who'd moved into Northern cities in the decades following the Civil War. She gathered a group of fifty women in the basement of the Bethel AME Church in Detroit, and together they strategized the boycotting of businesses that did not hire Black employees or that charged extremely high prices, particularly targeting the meatpacking industry; some accounts claimed that the group burned down a huge packinghouse. By 1935, there were more than ten thousand women members of what Peck had called Housewives Leagues in cities across the country, and thousands of members marched through Chicago, shutting down the whole meatpacking industry. The historian Stephen Tuck has argued that Peck "was a canny strategist" in that—despite being a successful mass organizer—she adopted "the nonthreatening posture of a group of housewives."

Presenting maternal morality, mothering instincts, and wifely responsibility as the motivator for female political participation permits it to exist without grave social penalty, but it can simultaneously hide the anger that so often drives that participation. The politicized female educators of the late nineteenth and early twentieth centuries, frustrated by the reduced educational opportunities for women and African Americans, would open, run, and teach at many of the public, women's, and historically Black colleges that would educate future generations; they pioneered new fields—such as teaching and nursing and social work—and later unionized and strategized alongside male-dominated unions to become politically powerful. The civic education schools started by Septima Clark in the Jim Crow South would become a training ground for many civil rights activists.

Female activists of what would become the civil rights movement not only organized marches and sit-ins; their thinking was fundamental to legal strategies for racial and gender equality. The civil rights lawyer Pauli Murray's writing on race, gender, and discrimination was so original and crucial that it would be cited by Supreme Court Justice Thurgood Marshall as the "bible for civil rights lawyers." Supreme Court Justice Ruth Bader Ginsburg credited Murray as one of the "brave women" whose intellectual efforts had been the basis for the sex discrimination protections Ginsburg was fighting for as a lawyer arguing in front of the Supreme Court in the decades before she was appointed as a justice.

Among the most activating moments of the early civil rights

movement was the 1955 murder of Emmett Till, a fourteen-year-old African American child from Chicago, who was beaten to death and left in a river after having been accused of flirting with a white woman while visiting an uncle in Mississippi. After his body was finally found, authorities tried to bury him in Mississippi without allowing his mother, Mamie, who was back in Chicago, to even look at him. "I don't know what authority [they] had to bury my son but [they] took that authority," Mamie Till recalled in a 2005 documentary. She insisted on having the casket delivered back to Chicago. Once there, the Chicago funeral director told her he had been prohibited from opening the box containing her son's body. Till recalled saying to the funeral director, "Do you have a hammer? . . . [Because] if you can't open the box, I can, and I'm going in the box."

The box was opened, and interviewed fifty years after the fact, Mamie Till was still driven to describe in detail what she saw as she gazed at her son's body: "I saw his tongue had been choked out and was lying down on his chin. I saw that his eye was out and was lying about midway to his cheek. I looked at this eye and it was gone. I looked at the bridge of his nose and it looked like someone had taken a meat chopper and chopped it. And I looked at his teeth because I took so much pride in his teeth . . . and I only saw two . . . They'd been just knocked out, and I was looking at his ears . . . and I didn't see the ear . . . . That's when I discovered a hole about here and I could see daylight on the other side . . . And I also discovered that they had taken an axe and they had gone straight down across his head and his face and the back of his head were separate."

When the funeral director asked if he should try to fix Emmett's features, Till replied, "No, let the people see what I've seen."

The people saw. More than fifty thousand of them saw Emmett's body—identifiable only because of a ring he wore—in person. They saw because Mamie Till, grieving the brutal murder of her child, insisted on having an open-casket funeral to which the public was invited. They saw because Mamie Till wanted the photos of his bloated, mutilated face to be published nationally in *Jet* magazine.

Mamie Till is credited as a transformative figure but is most often pictured as a grieving mother being held up at her son's coffin, weeping at his gravesite, supported and barely able to stand, her mouth open not in fury but in wailing loss. What we are never trained to consider is that alongside her sorrow and suffering was a burning rage. Mourning and sadness do not drive a woman to fight for her son's body, to vow to smash open his casket, to commit the crimes done to his body and face to eternal memory, to *make damn sure* that the world has to look at the same image of racist brutality that has been visited on her family and her life.

Anger does that. In the case of Mamie Till, anger lit a match under the civil rights struggle that would help to partially remake the United States and lessen (though not in any way eliminate) many of the legal and political obstacles to racial equality.

And we never think—have never been asked to think—of *her anger* as that righteous spark.

Keeping Cool

Keeping that anger simmering, remaining cool, or playing up other less threatening emotions, can be effective too, but is also part of the dynamic that leads us to ignore—to never even see—the power of women's rage, simply because if it is kept beneath the surface, even strategically, we never have to acknowledge its existence. It was the teachings of nonviolent protest techniques that led Rosa Parks—in the same year that Mamie Till forced the world to see what lynching looked like—to not give up her seat on a Montgomery bus in 1955. In the South, Jim Crow laws required Black men and women to sit at the back of buses, and if a white person boarded the bus and needed a seat, Black passengers had to give up their seats. At the end of a long day, the story goes, Parks was tired and refused to give up her seat. Her arrest prompted the Montgomery Bus Boycott, one of the earliest acts of nonviolent civil disobedience that ignited the civil rights movement. In truth, at the time of her arrest, Parks was already a leader within that movement, and her bus activism was not random, but planned long in advance.

Parks is widely remembered and celebrated as a civil rights heroine, but she is also memorialized as unemotional, pitied for having been exhausted, appreciated for her very refusal to show anger. But Parks was angry, and a lifelong furious fighter against racial violence and violence against women, even when she was a child.

At ten years old, she was threatened by a white boy, and she picked up a piece of brick and drew it back to strike him if he approached. "I was angry," she'd later say of that youthful act of resistance. "He went his way without further comment." Her sense of self-determination was nonnegotiable. "I would rather be lynched than live to be mistreated and not be allowed to say 'I don't like it.'" In her later life, Parks became interested in the Black power movement. Much of

Parks's activism against violence against women wasn't known to the general public until Danielle McGuire's 2010 book *At the Dark End of the Street*, and the intensity of her political investments was hidden beneath the sanitized, rage-free caricature of her circulated by the press and by the leaders of the very movement she helped to kick-start. But women within the civil rights movement, including activists Pauli Murray and Anna Arnold Hedgeman, were in turn angry at movement leaders who minimized Parks's role as an active, dynamic, driven political agitator, and many have strained since to offer a fuller and more complete picture of her.

"Dr. Martin Luther King, [Jr.] is the name most people associate with the Montgomery bus boycott," observed Angela Davis in *A Place of Rage*. "Of course Rosa Parks's name is known because she refused to sit in the back of the bus, but most often she is portrayed as someone who was not politically involved, who simply one day got tired of sitting in the back of the bus and refused to move. . . . Well of course she probably did get tired of sitting in the back of the bus. But that wasn't the reason why she refused to move to the back of the bus. That was a political act on her part."

There was another person who fought bus segregation in Montgomery whose activism and courage was forgotten for decades, and that may be *because* she didn't hold back. Nine months before Rosa Parks defied segregationist authority, fifteen-year-old Claudette Colvin unwittingly set the stage for the successful boycott to come, wrote Colvin's biographer Philip Hoose. And she did it because she was fuming mad.

On March 2, 1955, Colvin boarded the bus from school and sat in the middle section. There were no white people on the bus, and she was gazing out the window, not noticing as the bus began to fill up, until a white woman stood expectantly by her seat and the driver called for Colvin to get up. She stayed put. Police officers boarded the bus and grabbed her wrists, sending her schoolbooks to the floor; still she would not move. "History kept me stuck to my seat," Colvin would later recall. "I felt the hand of Harriet Tubman pushing down on one shoulder and Sojourner Truth pushing down on the other." She was dragged off the bus raging and screaming, handcuffed, and thrown into jail, where she wept for hours until her dad bailed her out.

A year later, as the official boycott was in full effect, Colvin risked her life to volunteer to testify in court in support of a lawsuit against the city's segregation laws. When the city lawyer demanded to know why she supported the bus boycott, she answered, "Because we were treated wrong, dirty and nasty." The incident and its aftermath were very hard on Colvin; she felt isolated and lost friends. There are debates about why Black civil rights leaders did not turn Colvin's arrest into the spark for their boycott, why they instead waited for Parks. One potential reason was that she was young and her anger seemed uncontrollable. "My generation was angry," she later said. She was considered a loose cannon who could not be trusted to maintain the necessary discipline for the long civil rights struggle.

Often, it was men within the movement who had the final say over a variety of decisions. The student activist and civil rights leader Diane Nash has recalled how when she was working to found the Student Nonviolent Coordinating Committee (SNCC) during the civil rights era of the 1960s, "there was a huge problem of good old boys getting together, and I was the only female in the group that was setting up SNCC originally. . . . Later on, in the Southern Christian Leadership Conference, black ministers dominated it. There was a great deal of misogyny there . . . it was expected that leadership would be male."

Civil rights leaders including Nash, Rosa Parks, Gloria Richardson, Dorothy Height, and Anna Arnold Hedgeman, who'd been charged with drawing thirty thousand white Protestants to attend the 1963 March on Washington, bristled during some of Martin Luther King Jr.'s speech that day, frustrated that women had been discouraged from giving speeches themselves, that they'd been instructed to march with the male leaders' wives, behind the men. Of the patriarchy within the civil rights movement, Height would later recall, "I've never seen a more immovable force. We could not get women's participation taken seriously." What she learned, she'd go on to say, was that if Black women "did not demand our rights, we were not going to get them." And Hedgeman would later warn, crisply, "The male would be better advised to spend less time mourning the loss of his superiority and more time working in partnership with women."

Black female civil rights activists faced indignities not only from patriarchal men in their movement, but also often condescension or erasure by white women.

Messy Coalition

In 1963 Betty Friedan, a white writer from the suburbs, published *The Feminine Mystique*, and it became a phenomenon that sparked the modern Second Wave women's movement by awakening a rage bubbling within. The book began: "The problem lay buried, unspoken, for many years in the minds of American women. It was a strange stirring, a sense of dissatisfaction, a yearning that women suffered in the middle of the twentieth century in the United States. Each suburban wife struggled with it alone. As she made the beds, shopped for groceries, matched slipcover material, ate peanut-butter sandwiches with her children, chauffeured Cub Scouts and Brownies, lay beside her husband at night, she was afraid to ask even of herself the silent question 'Is this all?'"

Friedan's address of the isolation, tedium, and suffocation of suburban white women within the homes of the white men in whom the government had invested so much power and authority would become politically revolutionary precisely *because* of the mass power of that numbed population that yearned to fulfill ambition outside the home. They desperately *needed* to be woken, for their dissatisfactions and stifled fury to be seen. Yet her book made no acknowledgment of Black women or their very relevant circumstances: That racism and its economic disadvantages meant that the majority of Black women in America had *always* had to work for wages.

In the 1930s, decades before Friedan published *The Feminine Mystique*, Black Philadelphia lawyer Sadie Alexander had written that "work for wages has always been more widespread among Negro than among white women," that the need to earn a living was particularly important for Black women, and suggested that this was, in fact, to the benefit of those women and their families and the world beyond. "The derogatory effects of the mother being out of the home are over balanced by the increased family income," Alexander wrote, going on to suggest that the positive impact of women taking themselves seriously as wage earners extended far beyond individual families. "The increased leisure that is enjoyed by women who have entered the industrial and manufacturing enterprises is giving rise to an improved educational and social standard among Negro women."

Alexander was concerned that women left their jobs at high rates because "women do not consider their jobs as permanent." Women were conditioned to anticipate family events that would take them out of workforces, Alexander argued, which made them "slow to organize in unions" and in turn made men "slower to accept them" as professional peers. Long before Friedan hit the scene with a volume aimed squarely and exclusively at middle-class white women, Alexander had been arguing for women's increased participation in the labor force, yet Friedan was the one hailed as "the mother of the [feminist] movement."

Some of this had to do with the fact that publishing houses and newspapers or magazines where such books were promoted were run by white people—mostly men—and there was little to no investment in spreading the experiences, writing, or accumulated wisdom of Black women. Part of the problem also stems from a white cultural understanding of whiteness as simply the norm, the standard against which everything else is a deviation, different—even if, as was often true, the innovation of nonwhite thinking had come before. The effect of these dynamics was the difficulty many white women have had in getting a firm view of the ways in which, even as they have been marginalized by men, they themselves have very often marginalized nonwhite women.

Writing at the start of her 1940 memoir, the civil rights and suffrage activist Mary Church Terrell described her story as one about "[a] colored woman living in a white world. It cannot possibly be like a story written by a white woman. A white woman has only one handicap to overcome—that of sex. I have two—both sex and race. I belong to the only group in this country which has two such huge obstacles to surmount. Colored men have only one—that of race." Terrell's is what the Rutgers women and gender studies professor Brittney Cooper has called "one of the earliest articulations of the political stakes of intersectionality," a term that would be coined by Kimberlé Williams Crenshaw nearly five decades later to describe the interlocking sets of biases faced by women of color in America. This was more than simply a doubling of bias; for the racism faced by nonwhite women is amplified and altered by sexism, and the sexism they encounter is twisted and worsened by racial bias.

In practice, these dynamics have long meant that Black women's expressions of frustration, resistance, or even mild critique have been exaggerated as some defining feature of Black femininity. And so, wrote Joelle Owusu in 2018, as a Black woman, she is regularly "perceived as the aggressor in every situation . . . Even when you are being polite and respectful during an altercation, someone will always make a remark about a black woman's 'attitude' or 'aggression.'"

These are the dynamics that the writer and philosopher Audre Lorde described in "The Uses of Anger," which is about women responding to racism, including the racism of other women, when she recalls "the most vocal white woman" responding to a weeklong forum on Black and white women by saying, "'I think I've gotten a lot. I feel black women really understand me a lot better now; they have a better idea of where I'm coming from.'" This, Lorde points out, is an example of the assumption that "understanding her"—the white woman—"lay at the core of the racist problem."

Women of color, and specifically Black women, are the demographic most likely to see their struggles as intertwined both with other women's and with Black men's, and to work alongside white women and Black men—often pioneering the thinking and doing the labor of organization central to movements for liberation and equality. Which makes it a terrific injustice that the movements to liberate women and African Americans have so often been understood as having been led by white women and Black men. They are understood this way because white supremacy and patriarchy permit white women and Black men greater access to money, and more contact with the media that covers social movements and the politicians who respond to them, than Black women have.

There is indeed an argument that the women's movement has survived over centuries not in spite of but *because of* its messiness: because the women of color who have pushed the movement from the inside, forcing it to grow and change and be better—even when they haven't always agreed on what better meant—have helped it meet the shifting forms and expressions of inequity from era to era.

Audre Lorde argued that the honest expression of anger between women of different races is necessary if coalition building is ever going to happen, to tear down walls that divide us into competing camps, which serve only to uphold patriarchal power: "For black women and white women to face one another's angers without denial or immobility or silence or guilt" can breathe life into the movement for women's equality and freedom, she wrote. "It implies peers meeting upon a common basis to examine difference[s], and to alter those distortions which history has created around our difference. For it is those distortions which separate us. And we must ask ourselves: Who profits from all this?" The answer is usually the white male minority already in power. The angers between women, Lorde argued, "can transform difference[s] through insight into power. For anger between peers births change, not destruction, and the discomfort and sense of loss it often causes is not fatal, but a sign of growth." As women recognize the contributions and struggles of one another, which sometimes are conveyed through anger, they recognize the power that they have in coalition to break the tyranny of the patriarchal structures holding all of them down.

Backlash Backfired

By the mid-1960s, the stuffing of middle-class American women back into the box of early marital expectation and domestic confinement—a box that chafed all the more thanks to the revolutionary opportunities that had so recently been made available to their mothers and grandmothers—had created a world so airless that it was nearly destined to combust, more forcefully than ever before. And the mounting pressure for civil rights laws that recognized the humanity and dignity of African Americans grew so intense that white men in power were finally forced to relent.

In 1964, after decades of strategic, angry but nonviolent struggle by activists from all walks and stages of life, President Lyndon Johnson signed the landmark Civil Rights Act. It stated that all people "shall be entitled to the full and equal enjoyment of the goods, services, facilities, and privileges, advantages, and accommodations of any place of public accommodation . . . without discrimination or segregation on the ground of race, color, religion, or national origin." The following year, at the urging of civil rights leaders, he signed into law the 1965 Voting Rights Act, which outlawed racial discrimination in laws governing voting.

Segregation and discrimination were no longer legal anywhere in the land. Moving forward, the struggle was to make sure the law would be enforced so that women could experience true equal treatment under the law. And angry women would continue to be at the forefront of these battles.

· 6 ·

Second Wave

A few years ago I sat at a family holiday table listening to my mother and my aunt tell stories of their early days in academia, in the 1960s and early 1970s. Sisters from a farm in northern Maine, both women went on to get PhDs from the same graduate school and go into the same field. My mother, just five years older than my aunt, recalled going on the job market after earning her degree and seeing interview postings that read "We will not be hiring a woman for this position." At one interview, she was told as she walked in the door, "We're not considering women, but I thought it was unfair that they didn't get practice interviewing, so you can have a trial run." At another, she was told, "You're very good, but we already have one of you in the department." By the time her sister came along, just five years later, these hiring practices were not only frowned upon, they were illegal.

They were illegal in part because in those intervening years women, mad at how they were discriminated against and harassed, had expressed their fury and had brought lawsuits, thanks to the Civil Rights Act of 1964. Some women had become lawyers themselves, and some of these, including Eleanor Holmes Norton and Ruth Bader Ginsburg, went to work advocating for women. Holmes Norton led the establishment of laws barring harassment of women in the workplace and later became the single delegate to the US Congress from Washington, DC. Ginsburg brought an array of legal cases that fought gender discrimination to court, and she ultimately rose to be appointed to a seat on the US Supreme Court by President Bill Clinton in 1993. A willingness to be mad as hell and pick strategic fights changed the legal system and changed laws, altering the professional landscape for my aunt, in ways that would have been inconceivable to even her older sister.

In many ways, the uprising of women of the Second Wave mass feminist movement during the 1960s and 1970s was tackling the same laundry list of inequities laid out in the Declaration of Sentiments of 1848. In part this was because while the women of the late 1800s and early 1900s had succeeded in expanding educational and professional opportunities and altering some property laws, the major win, more than seventy years after the Declaration's composition, had been the Nineteenth Amendment to the US Constitution giving women the right to vote. In the 1960s women still could not get credit cards in their own name, serve on juries in every state, have their sports funded equally in schools, or get an abortion. So much was still left to be done, and righteous anger fueled women for the fight, but it didn't always come easily.

People often consider Gloria Steinem—white, cisgender, traditionally feminine and foxy—as the great communicator of this era's feminist rage. In the early 1970s, she was feminism's new and powerful popularizer, a woman who would come to stand (insufficiently and often to her own dismay) for the diverse, noisy, flawed, and multifaceted movement whose sometimes spiky messages she was so capable of transmitting smoothly to the broader public. But Steinem described to me the lifelong process of learning to feel, recognize, acknowledge, and express her own anger in real time. Her mother had given up a career as a journalist to raise children and then suffered a mental illness that left her daughters as her caretakers. But raised in the mid-twentieth-century era of domestic repression, Steinem was taught to resist anger. For a while, she said, she "transplanted [her] anger, which is not uncommon for women to do, into other things." She could be angry at anyone who treated an animal badly, or another person, but not angry on her own behalf.

When she was in her thirties and a working journalist, she was sent to cover a hearing on abortion. It was 1969, and ending a pregnancy was still illegal. As Steinem recalled, "I'm sure that [anger is] what I felt at the first abortion hearing, the moment when I suddenly realized that *yes*, I had had an abortion, and so had one in three other women [but that it was illegal]. I'm sure what I felt was anger: *How is this okay? This is completely irrational!* I was fueled by anger." That fuel propelled her into the women's movement. Still, she said, for many years "I could finally tell people on a Thursday that I'd been angry on Monday. I couldn't tell them in real time." Even with half a century as a feminist organizer and women's leader under her belt, as a woman who understands that "anger is great fuel for political activism; it's wonderful and I value it, I treasure it"—still, she said, to this day she can express anger in real time "only occasionally."

During her decades in the spotlight, the media regularly, and hungrily, positioned her as perhaps the *only* feminist that America was interested in hearing from. But on the road, she said, where she spoke regularly with fellow activist Florynce Kennedy—an unapologetic source of frank fury—"I always had to speak first because if I went after Flo, it was such an anticlimax. There was no question, I had to go first."

Flo Kennedy's life was a study in unapologetic and furious resistance to injustice. As a young woman in Kansas City, Missouri, she had participated in a boycott of a nearby Coca-Cola bottling company that did not hire African American truck drivers. When she was denied entry to Columbia Law School—not because she was Black but because she was a woman, administrators told her—she threatened a discrimination lawsuit and was admitted, as one of eight women, and the only African American, in her class. As a lawyer, she represented members of the Black Panther Party, an organization that advocated for social justice, equal rights, and political power for Black Americans, against charges of conspiracy to commit bombings. She also sued the Catholic Church and in 1969 organized feminist legal objection to New York State's abortion ban, which was overturned in 1970. Kennedy was in the cast of the 1983 feminist movie *Born in Flames*, about revolutionary women who band together in a rebel army to battle gender and racial oppression.

Kennedy was described by *People* magazine as having "the biggest, loudest, and, indisputably, the rudest mouth on the battleground where feminist activists and radical politics join in mostly common cause." When they were on the speaking circuit as partners, Steinem recalled being scolded by Kennedy for being a Goody Two-shoes, too afraid to yell and get emotional, and instead behaving like the journalist she'd started as and relying too heavily on data in her speeches. "In the beginning I remember her taking me aside, because I was into facts and figures—I felt I had to prove that we were discriminated against. And Flo hauled me off and said, 'Honey, when you are lying in a ditch with a truck on your ankle, you do not send someone to the library to find out how much the truck weighs. You get it off!'"

But even if Kennedy was rhetorically tireless in her anger, her dynamism wasn't always embraced by those in the movement. Steinem recalled inviting Kennedy to speak in Washington at a big women's organizing meeting. "Tons of people were coming from all over, in complete disorganization, and I invited Flo," Steinem recalled. "I remember Betty Friedan calling me up, furious, saying, 'You cannot invite her, you cannot have her there,'" because she thought Kennedy was too militant. Steinem ignored Friedan. Kennedy came and spoke at the meeting, "and of course it was fine." More than fine. Along with Kennedy's rage burned an "incredible generosity" and good humor, Steinem recalled. "The classic Flo line," said Steinem, who was Kennedy's regular speaking partner, "was when some guy in the back got up and asked us 'Are you lesbians?' and she responded 'Are you my alternative?'" Kennedy, said Steinem, "could always say something that made people laugh. But it always had a point. I mean, she was not letting anybody off the hook by making people laugh."

In the hand-wringing over the dangers of feeling too much rage, or the idea that to be angry is to be prickly, inhospitable, aggressive, what's often missed is that the release of anger can accompany, and perhaps prompt, joy, goodwill, warmth, and kindness. "Flo was very accepting of the idea that people are activists in a lot of different ways and that's okay," Steinem remembered. But Kennedy's willingness to unleash anger—the impulse that is so scorned in some women—was also a habit that inspired (if occasionally terrified) so many others.

"A big reason it's very important for women in public life to be able to express anger on behalf of all of us who feel it [is] so that we can have a champion," said Steinem, recalling another friend and contemporary, the throaty, tough-talking fireplug of a New York congresswoman, Bella Abzug. At the 1977 Women's Conference in Houston, at which Maxine Waters, then a thirty-nine-year-old state assemblywoman from California, was waiting to talk to Abzug, Steinem recalled, "Bella was yelling at me, screaming at me something like 'You've ruined everything!'" Steinem remembered noticing Waters watching her argument with Abzug. "I could see that Maxine was appalled. So I took Maxine aside and said, 'This is just the way we talk to each other in New York. Don't worry about it.'" But however startling her gruffness, Steinem continued, "Bella could be our champion. I mean, she pushed some people away, but the people *loved* her for getting angry. Flo too. Flo could be our champion."

Kennedy's close friend, the former New York Supreme Court judge Emily Jane Goodman, said at the time of Kennedy's death in 2000 that Kennedy "showed a whole generation of us the right way to live our lives." The exuberance of Kennedy's rage was contagious. Here was a model of righteous female fury who people wanted to be near. But as colorful, clever, and crackling as Flo Kennedy was, it remained an uphill battle to get people in power (still mostly men) to take the so-called women's issues she championed seriously.

In 1972, Shirley Chisholm—the first Black woman ever elected to Congress—ran for the presidency and made it all the way to the Democratic National Convention, where delegates would select the party's nominee for the presidency, the Democrat who would face Republican President Richard Nixon in the fall. Chisholm, then in her second congressional term, had already worked to expand the food stamp program to pay for groceries for people who could not afford them as well as the Special Supplemental Nutrition Program for Women, Infants, and Children, which provided funds for parents to buy food and baby formula for their children; she had pushed a $10 billion bill to help families pay for childcare, a version of which was passed by Congress before President Nixon vetoed it. She was also an outspoken supporter of women's rights to have full autonomy over their bodies, including the right to end a pregnancy.

The party's national convention in 1972 was a wild one, thanks in no small part to the participation of the National Women's Political Caucus, which had been founded the previous year by Chisholm, Flo Kennedy, and other feminists and civil rights leaders including Steinem, Friedan, and Dorothy Height. In Miami, they convened and argued: over Chisholm's candidacy; over the eventual nominee, George McGovern; over the Equal Rights Amendment; and over a controversial abortion plank proposed for the party's platform. And as it was all unfolding, they got almost no television coverage.

This led Kennedy and a group of other women that included Sandra Hochman—a white feminist poet who had been given $15,000 by independent film producers to make a documentary about feminists at the convention—to storm the TV crews and reporters gathered on the convention's floor during a down moment. Kennedy, enormous peace-sign earrings flying, was aiming all her ire at a bunch of white broadcast news journalists who were taking a break on the mostly empty convention floor; for the most part, the men were showing little interest in Kennedy's fury. The powerful newsmen sat, silent and amused, some not looking up from their newspapers, as the scrum of women confronted them. The women's fury only built in response to the men's inattention and bubbled over at the couple of guys who tried to hush them. When one of the men tried to persuade Kennedy to back away, pushing her aside, she blew up at them, yelling at them profanely to take their hands off her.

Hochman's camera crew had recorded it all for her documentary, which would be called *Year of the Woman*. The film captured so much of the gendered scorn and dismissal that was provoking those women to scream their heads off: footage of the news crews who wouldn't cover Chisholm; a Democratic power broker telling Hochman that there *were* women working on George McGovern's campaign, "so far mostly in the childcare centers and things like that"; McGovern's dashing young campaign manager, Gary Hart, then two years away from his own bid for the US Senate, telling Hochman that his boss wouldn't pick a female vice presidential candidate because there was no "satisfactory woman candidate . . . qualified to be president of the United States."

Hochman's movie played for five nights in New York City's Greenwich Village to sold-out crowds in 1973, and then, except for a handful of screenings, mostly disappeared from public view for forty-two years. When I saw it years later, I immediately understood what had made it so charged and dangerous, what had made it *too much*: It was a wholly unfiltered view of women's outrage.

"We are people that have been left out!" Hochman shouts in the film, and it's hard to disagree with her frustration, although it's also hard not to notice that she is wearing a papier-mâché crocodile mask while screaming. "People don't take women seriously. They make them into freaks. So I say, as a poet, be a freak." The whole documentary is filled with women activists acting like freaks: wearing sparkly eyeglass frames, snorkeling masks, and Mickey Mouse ears.

This view—of anger burning raw and hot, crude and freakish; of the men who controlled the national popular narrative about women, politics, and power, who tried to get Flo Kennedy to stop yelling by putting their hands on her—brought a jolting realization when I first saw it a few years ago that the freakishness was, as Hochman noted, a by-product of unfiltered fury. A desperate *rage* at being manhandled, ignored, sidelined, and not taken seriously was driving this group of revolutionaries—some of them leading public figures in the still-growing Second Wave feminist movement—to behave outlandishly. Their frustration at the seeming impossibility of their project was being let loose, overtaking common sense about polite discussion. They would do *anything* to get people to hear how livid they were, lizard cosplay its own furious reflection of the amusement and contempt with which these powerful men regarded them.

The smear that a woman who is angry is also *unstable* is cast every day in popular political chatter, so often we probably don't understand how completely we absorb the connection. The idea that women's anger is fundamentally illegitimate, because they have nothing *real*, no big things to be rationally angry about, supports the notion that furious women are mentally ill. As Kennedy wrote in her memoir, "I'm just a loudmouthed, middle-aged colored lady with a fused spine and three feet of intestines missing, and a lot of people think I'm crazy. Maybe you do too, but I never stop to wonder why I'm not like other people. The mystery to me is why more people aren't like me."

• 7 •

Constant Pushing

Shirley Chisholm's groundbreaking race for the White House inspired many women to tap into their inner rage at injustice and discrimination and pursue politics. One of those women was Barbara Lee.

Barbara Lee was born in Texas in 1946, almost two decades before the passage of the Civil Rights Act and the Voting Rights Act, to a mother who was always straightforward about her anger. "She didn't take any prisoners," said Lee. "She was really upfront about inappropriate speech and behavior. She didn't mince her words; she wouldn't take any mess." Lee recalled a story her mother had relayed about how, as a college student, she and a friend had wanted to join Alpha Kappa Alpha, the nation's first Black sorority. Back then, AKA admitted only light-skinned women like Lee's mother. "So my grandmother looked like she was white, and my mother was very fair with green eyes," said Lee. But the sorority turned down her mother's best friend Juanita, whose skin was darker. "My mother got furious," said Lee. "She said 'To hell with this; I'm not joining,'" and called on the civil rights activist and educator Mary McLeod Bethune to come down to Texas Southern University and help students organize in protest. "That's how my mother was," Lee said. "She was constantly pushing."

When Lee herself was a high school student in San Fernando, California, she wanted to be a cheerleader, but the school had never had a Black cheerleader, in part because of the way those choosing who would be selected kept their process hidden behind closed doors. "I was mad," recalled Lee of her teenage self, "because I knew all these white girls had had the opportunity to be cheerleaders, and I knew I couldn't." In those years, the National Association for the Advancement of Colored People (NAACP) worked all around the country to press for equal rights for Black Americans by pushing for civil rights laws and bringing lawsuits that fought the discrimination Black people faced. "So I went to the NAACP out of anger and asked them if they could help me and they said yeah." Lee and her classmates staged protests to change the rules, ensuring that girls could try out in front of the student body. Lee became the first Black cheerleader at San Fernando High, and was soon joined on the squad by an Asian American student. "That was anger," she said. "I was *really* angry. I voiced my anger. But I was strategic, and I got what I wanted, not just for me but for everybody else, for all these girls of color who wanted to be cheerleaders."

In her early twenties, Lee was a student at Mills College in California; she was by then a single mother of two sons and living in poverty. "I was angry at the system of oppression and racism because I saw it, I lived it every day, and who wouldn't be angry? I was being dissed by social workers and jerked around by guys and all that stuff." She became the head of the campus Black Student Union and started doing community work with the Black Panther Party. "I wanted to make whatever intervention I could to make things better for other people." But her interventions did not include electoral politics; she had no interest in working within the American political system. Lee's lack of belief in the system was hurting her grades; as a government major, she was required to do fieldwork for a campaign, but she was not even registered to vote in early 1972.

That's when Shirley Chisholm came to speak at Mills College as part of her presidential campaign. Lee attended the speech and listened as Chisholm spoke to students in fluent Spanish; she talked about health care, poverty, women's rights, racial justice, and immigrants' rights. Lee couldn't believe it. She approached Chisholm afterward and suggested that she'd like to work on her campaign in the California primary, confessing that she'd previously not had anything to do with electoral politics. Chisholm, Lee recalled, "Shook her finger at me. 'Little girl!'—I was twenty-five! I had two little kids, they were probably with me!—But anyway, she said 'Little girl! If you really believe in what you stand for, then you'll register to vote, get involved with politics, and try to make change. Because we need you.'"

Lee did register to vote and wound up organizing Chisholm's Northern California campaign with other local college students and attending the Democratic National Convention in Miami as a Chisholm delegate. Years later, Lee won a seat in the US Congress, serving the people of Oakland, California; she was their congresswoman for over twenty years. And in that capacity, she told me, "I've learned how to . . . I won't even say *finesse* it, but how to handle life without going ballistic every time I feel like I'm treated unjustly, or other people are treated unjustly."

For women in public life, especially those engaged in a fight for more equal opportunities for more kinds of people, the message has long been clear: Their anger and desire to challenge the system—ironically, perhaps the thing that motivated their engagement in social change and political life to begin with—will be used against them no matter how it is expressed.

Hot Tears of Anger

By the late sixties, women's anger had led to entirely new forms of civil disobedience: In 1965, a University of Chicago student named Heather Booth helped a friend's sister get an illegal abortion. When other women began to call for help, she and a group of young feminists developed an elaborate system of phone numbers, code words, and houses that would be known as the Jane Collective; they would assist more than eleven thousand women in getting safe abortions between 1969 and 1973 so that those women were not forced to remain pregnant against their will.

The fight for reproductive control was a crucial part of the feminist movement in the 1960s and early 1970s, as women became more driven to exert authority over their own bodies, sexuality, and structure of their families.

"The question," Chisholm had declared in 1969, "is not: can we justify abortions, but can we justify compulsory pregnancy?" She had recently been named the first honorary co-president of NARAL, an abortion rights organization. She was both frank and morally assured in the remarks she delivered to the Republican Task Force on Earth Resources and Population, asking pointedly, "What is more immoral, granting an abortion or forcing a young girl . . . to assume the responsibilities of an adult while she is still a child?"

At that messy 1972 presidential convention, the eventual Democratic presidential candidate, George McGovern, would persuade many of the feminists who'd attended to back him (over Chisholm, one of their own) by appearing to promise that he'd support legalizing abortion in his party's platform. But after Chisholm surrendered her delegates, McGovern double-crossed the feminists, instructing his delegates not to support the legalization of abortion and violating a further promise to the women by permitting an antiabortion activist to speak from the convention floor. The journalist (and later screenwriter) Nora Ephron covered the messy convention for *Esquire*: At four o'clock in the morning, Ephron wrote, Gloria Steinem "in tears, was confronting McGovern campaign manager Gary Hart: 'You promised us you would not take the low road, you bastards.'"

The next day, Ephron trailed Steinem out of a hotel where she'd gone to speak to McGovern directly but hadn't succeeded. Steinem seethed to Ephron, walking away from the hotel and starting to cry again. "It's just that they won't take us seriously," Steinem told Ephron through tears. "And I'm just tired of being screwed, and being screwed by my friends. By George McGovern, whom I raised half the money for in his first campaign, wrote his speeches . . . he just doesn't understand. We went to see him at one point about abortion, and the question of welfare came up. 'Why are you concerned about welfare?' he said. He didn't understand it was a woman's issue. They won't take us seriously. We're just walking wombs."

Steinem's tirade, as recorded forever by Ephron, was a righteous rant, months and years of fury spilling over, and she couldn't get it out without weeping. "We cry when we get angry," Steinem said to me forty-five years later, recalling the conversation and still shaking her head with some apparent regret that she'd wept, and that Ephron had caught her at it. "I don't think that's uncommon, do you? That women cry when we get angry?" That Steinem would look for reassurance on this point is stunning in itself: Of course women cry when they get angry. But she continued, "I was greatly helped by a woman who was an executive someplace, who said she also cried when she got angry, but developed a technique which meant that when she got angry and started to cry, she'd say to the person she was talking to, 'You may think I am sad because I am crying. No. I am angry.' And then she just kept going. And I thought that was brilliant."

Tears are one of the most frequent outlets for our wrath in part because they are fundamentally misunderstood. One of my sharpest memories from an early job, in a male-dominated office where I too once found myself weeping with inexpressible rage, was being grabbed by the scruff of my neck by an older woman—a chilly, hard-charging manager of whom I'd always been slightly terrified—who dragged me into a stairwell. "Never let them see you crying," she told me. "They don't know you're furious. They think you're sad and will be pleased because they got to you."

Congresswoman Barbara Lee recalled to me, a century later, how Chisholm herself, "cried behind closed doors when she was hurt. You know how pain leads to anger." In public, Lee recalled, Chisholm would be "so cool, her voice and demeanor tough and strong and *boom, boom, boom*. But get her behind closed doors? She'd let her guard down and acknowledge her pain." Lee recalled Chisholm's propensity for tears as a product of her being "very sensitive, very hurt, and very angry."

"Remember," Lee told me, "she was the only Black woman with all these men, white and Black. You come into an environment that is really the deck stacked against you: You're Black and you're a woman. I remember she'd say, 'Barbara, these rules weren't made for you or me.'" Lee remembered Chisholm as equally sensitive to the slights of the Congressional Black Caucus and her white colleagues in the women's movement. "Shirley was very clear that the white feminist movement did not understand the nature of racism and what Black women and Black people have to deal with. And she was equally angry at a lot of the African American leadership, because she didn't think they understood how women were being treated." And so, while Lee emphasized that Chisholm "never let anyone break her down in public," in private, she cried.

There is another dimension to the choice that many women make to cry: the fact that this emblem of helpless suffering provokes a sympathetic and protective response, mostly when the tears are being shed by white women. The protection those tears are understood to invite has often been used as the justification for racial violence. "White women's tears" have derailed important conversations about race, provoking sympathy for and connection with *some* kinds of women, but not others. "Not all tears matter," observed the writer Shay Stewart-Bouley in 2018. "Rarely do the tears of a nonwhite woman carry any value. . . . The damsel in distress is never Black."

And of course, she is very often envisioned as straight and cisgender.

Stonewall

Lots of people were gathered inside a bar in lower Manhattan in the early morning hours of June 28, 1969. In the years since, there have been angry disputes over who was inside, who was outside, who said what or threw what and at what time. But what is clear is that the Stonewall Inn, a dingy establishment that had no running water, was the rare gay bar in New York City that permitted dancing, and that it had become a mecca not only for gay men, but also for drag queens, trans people, some lesbians, sex workers, and homeless youth. It was a bar for the particularly marginalized, in a city and an era that already marginalized homosexuality in any form. Police raids on gay establishments were a regular occurrence, and cops often forced trans patrons to go to the bathrooms and reveal their private parts to them; at the time, "impersonating" a member of another gender was illegal in New York City, dressing in fewer than three pieces of gender-appropriate clothing was considered grounds for arrest.

Historians and participants may still disagree about exactly what happened in 1969, but in most recollections of the night, cross-dressers, drag queens, and a handful of lesbians were probably at the center of events. Marsha P. Johnson, an African American trans drag performer, was celebrating at the bar. A butch lesbian named Stormé DeLarverie was there; Sylvia Rivera, a trans gay rights activist, was outside on the street.

When the cops raided the Stonewall Inn that night, patrons were not in the mood to comply. Because they resisted, the raid took a long time, and onlookers and friends began to gather in large numbers outside. By some accounts, Johnson was among the first to resist inside the bar, throwing a shot glass and shouting, "I got my civil rights"; many agree that it was DeLarverie who pushed back hard at cops, cursing and angrily complaining about her handcuffs being too tight as she was led out of the bar. When cops put her in a police car, DeLarverie is reported to have shouted at the staring, sympathetic crowd, "Why don't you guys do something?"

It's at this point that Rivera, perhaps, threw a bottle at police, and others threw pennies, and the crowd outside rushed toward the paddy wagon containing those who'd already been arrested. Soon bricks, bottles, and glasses were flying, and the crowd outside launched an attack on the officers still in the bar, throwing rocks through its windows, pulling a parking meter from the street, and using it as a battering ram. As Rivera would recall later in life, the resistant fury that overtook the crowd and patrons of Stonewall felt like this: "You've been treating us like [garbage] all these years? Uh-huh. Now it's our turn!" She would also remember it as "one of the greatest moments in my life."

The so-called Stonewall Riots would last for days and mark the start of the gay liberation movement. Johnson and Rivera would go on to found and be active in the Gay Liberation Front, and together found STAR, the Street Transvestite Action Revolutionaries, dedicated to supporting homeless drag queens and trans people of color. DeLarverie was described in her *New York Times* obituary as, in her post-Stonewall years, having walked the streets of lower Manhattan, "like a gay superhero . . . She was not to be messed with by any stretch of the imagination."

DeLarverie would also later insist that the events of those nights be spoken about with care, and is reported to have framed them consciously as righteous political action. "It was a rebellion, it was an uprising, it was a civil rights disobedience," she reportedly told a symposium of Stonewall veterans. "It wasn't no damn riot."

But the angry women and gender nonconformists who were likely at the heart of that rebellion were very often erased from its retelling, and from the popular view of the gay rights movement, a movement so often embodied by the wealthy straight white men who were its most public figures. When, in 2015, Hollywood released its big film about the movement, *Stonewall*, focusing on the events at the Stonewall Inn, it did not star trans women, drag queens, lesbians, or nonwhite gender nonconformists as its heroes. Rather it was a fictionalized story of a young white cisgender man from the Midwest, the figure who could most comfortably be cast as the first to hurl a brick through a window and yell, "Gay power!"

• 8 •

Reactionary Politics

Rethinking Marriage, Again

The activists of the 1960s and 1970s led a revolutionary movement that lasted a few decades, but in that time, the resulting changes to American society dramatically altered the dynamics of home life. The Second Wave feminist movement challenged the historically inequitable assumptions about what made a family (straight couples only, patriarchal structure) and called into question how power and responsibility might be distributed within it.

The effect of this kind of social action—taking place in private as well as public spheres—was unsettling to men in ways that felt particularly intimate. Many men were suddenly experiencing pushback for behaviors and attitudes that had never before been presented as problematic. Some felt that they had entered marriages with a shared set of expectations but that the upheaval of the Second Wave had very suddenly destroyed those expectations.

As Stephanie Coontz, who has written about the history of marriage, has pointed out, "Feminism didn't make good marriages go bad." But it did challenge men to be better and offered women the opportunity to plan their lives around ambitions and desires not directly tied to husbands, because with more equality to pursue an advanced degree or get a well-paying job, women did not have to depend on their husbands to survive. These opportunities for escape and for alternate paths were, in fact, similar to what suffragists like Elizabeth Cady Stanton and Lucretia Mott had been clamoring for in the 1848 Declaration of Sentiments, what marriage reformers had been speaking about for more than a century.

Cecile Richards, the former president of the women's medical care organization Planned Parenthood (yes, the Planned Parenthood that was founded by Margaret Sanger in 1916), has written of how her progressive dad, a lawyer who'd fought on behalf of labor unions and for voting and civil rights, was undone by the changes brought by the women's movement. Cecile's equally progressive mother, Ann, had experienced a change during the 1970s, campaigning on behalf of the Equal Rights Amendment (ERA). Her father, Richards remembered, was confused. "He had a wife who raised the kids, took care of every single dog and cat we brought home, threw dinner parties, and grew organic vegetables," wrote Richards. "Dad had grown up—and was living in a household where women threw themselves into volunteer work and didn't have careers. I realize now that for him (and so many other men of his generation) the prospect of total upheaval of the domestic scene must have seemed pretty frightening. Suddenly the tumult around women's roles and aspirations wasn't happening just on television; it was happening in our own home." The Richardses' marriage, like so many of the era, ended in divorce. And Cecile's mom, Ann, went on to be elected governor of Texas.

Esther Kaplan, an editor of the Investigative Fund at the Nation Institute, told me that she frequently thought about how women in the 1960s and 1970s—the years of Second Wave feminism—had gathered together in suburban homes and city apartments, had talked about liberation and equality and sexuality. They had learned to look at their own bodies and lives in new ways, to recognize how their home lives subjugated them under the control of men, to question what they'd always been taught to accept as just the way things were.

"Those women *left their husbands*," Esther marveled to me, noting with wonder that "social movements have the potential to radically change us, not just radically change the world." "This kind of thing can be culturally explosive, radical, out of control." She meant this, and I understood it, positively. But for some, the eruptive velocity is too much.

She's right that fury can topple institutions, cut through our bedrock assumptions, and remake the geography of possibility. Not only did the consciousness raising of the 1970s result in a massive spike in the divorce rate, it also created a next generation that wanted to avoid the pitfalls of broken marriages that their parents had experienced, a population of women who expected more from the institution and so delayed marriage, or didn't marry at all, and instead expanded the possibilities for women to enjoy economic and social independence. Those women's lives were remapped. Generations of women moved forward at new speed, their dependency not just on marriage but on men wholly revised. The anger of the Second Wavers, anger that has been used to caricature them as unappealing, had blown off the doors for their daughters and their granddaughters.

Audre Lorde famously argued in her essay "The Uses of Anger" that "every woman has a well-stocked arsenal of anger potentially useful against those oppressions, personal and institutional, which brought that anger into being. Focused with precision it can become a powerful source of energy, serving progress and change." Lorde was very firm that she did not mean temporary, cosmetic change, not simply "the ability to smile or feel good." Rather, she argued, well-aimed anger from women can lead to "a basic and radical alteration in those assumptions underlining our lives."

It was surely not entirely fun to live through the era of quickly disintegrating marriages, though it is crucial to acknowledge that it was *also* not fun to live through eras in which divorce was hard to obtain, and marriages, even abusive and unhappy ones, were not easy for women to leave. (Remember how, in the 1900s, it felt more practical to ban alcohol than to remake a legal system that would give women equal power within marriages?) But the swiftness of this new feminist rupture of marital expectations meant that the divorce wave was fast and big and produced many painful splits; lots of kids suffered for it, lots of women and lots of men suffered through it. The chaos provoked by the divorce boom fueled an extremely effective antifeminist line: that feminists, in their political aims, were enemies of family, men, and marriage.

"If there's one thing feminists love, it's divorce," said Phyllis Schlafly, leader of the 1970s antifeminist crusade to stop the ratification of the ERA. What she did not acknowledge, of course, was that what feminists loved was equality of the sexes, and that the divorces that happened during the course of and in the wake of the Second Wave often were provoked by women's refusal to remain legally bound to men who did not want to have equal partnerships. Or by the realization that if they could get economic security on their own, by getting good jobs in industries that had formerly excluded them, they did not *need* to stay in marriages that didn't make them happy, or in which they were treated badly. And of course, Schlafly did not acknowledge the irony that while she was out crusading against equal rights for women, someone was at home cooking dinner for her family and taking care of her kids, and that someone often was not her.

And yet, whether due to timing, exhaustion, or other factors, the politics of people like Schlafly began to take center stage. The years following the great social movements of the twentieth century—the women's movement, the civil rights movement, the LGBTQ+ rights movement—were shaped by deeply reactionary politics, yet another backlash provoked by the fears of cultural change that these movements ushered in. When Phyllis Schlafly finally succeeded in killing the ERA in 1982, it was a sign that the Second Wave feminist movement of the 1970s, and the righteous fury that had ignited it, was losing strength.

Muffling Women's Rage—Again

In the 1980s, when Republican Ronald Reagan was president, an increasingly right-wing reactionary politics joined with religious conservatism, giving rise to a cultural backlash that hit back at all sorts of social progress. Right-wing and Republican politicians attacked the benefits, rights, and protections that gave poor women free or low-cost medical care, assistance paying for housing, and money for food so that they could support themselves and their families. They also went after women's reproductive freedom.

In 1970, New York had decriminalized abortion for any reason prior to the twenty-fourth week of pregnancy, and activists won similar victories in Washington, Alaska, and Hawaii with support from both political parties. In 1973, the Supreme Court had handed down a surprise decision legalizing abortion nationwide in the case of *Roe v. Wade*. Earlier in his political career, when he was governor of California, Reagan had signed what was at the time one of the country's most liberal abortion laws, permitting "therapeutic" abortions in cases of rape, incest, and threat to the life of the mother.

But by the time Reagan won the White House in 1980, the political parties had become more rigidly divided on the topic. Democrats were largely "pro-choice," supporting women's rights to choose to have abortions, and Republicans called themselves "pro-life," opposing a woman's right to abortion. Republicans had discovered that right-wing religious activists were highly motivated in their opposition to abortion and that constricting abortion rights by any and all means was a way to capture and engage those voters. And so Republicans began working every anti-abortion angle they could think of, building spidery networks of local and state anti-abortion lawmakers and creating a judicial pipeline of anti-abortion judges through the Federalist Society, an organization of right-wing legal professionals. Republicans dreamed up ever more imaginative laws that shut down abortion and family planning clinics based on building-code requirements related to hallway width—details that had nothing to do with the safety or effectiveness of abortion care, but worked as a roundabout way to outlaw it. Republican lawmakers enforced waiting periods to slow down pregnant women who sought to end their pregnancies and circulated literature making fictionalized claims about links between cancer and abortion. Republicans used the House floor in the US Congress as a stage to vote again and again to defund Planned Parenthood, even though it was already against the law for federal funds to pay for abortions, to send a dramatic public message to the people most motivated to organize for them.

The rising right-wing cultural wave also washed over parts of the women's movement that had produced legal, professional, and educational gains for middle-class women, better enabling them to live independently, outside of marriage, the patriarchal institution that had historically limited them and on which they long had had to depend. A 1986 *Newsweek* cover story blared the news that a single woman at forty was more likely to get killed by a terrorist than get married. That story was later proven to be false, and it would later become a key episode in Susan Faludi's 1991 book, *Backlash*, in which she tracked the varied, suffocating ways women's anger was muffled throughout the Reagan years: how feminist activism was blamed for a "man shortage," how the day care that enabled women to work outside the home was vilified as dangerous for children.

It was in this context that Democratic Congresswoman Patricia Schroeder from Colorado decided to run for president. She was working as the chair of Senator Gary Hart's presidential campaign in 1987 when the married Hart was caught in an extramarital affair. Schroeder, angry with Hart and deeply frustrated by the situation, thought, "Well, I've been going out and doing appearances for him, engaging in some debates." She decided that with her candidate out of the race, there was no reason that she shouldn't explore the idea of running for president herself.

"It was not a well-thought-out decision," she said to me with a laugh thirty years later. "There were already seven other candidates in the race, and the last thing they needed was another one. Somebody called it *Snow White and the Seven Dwarfs*." She understood that because she was a late entry, she was behind on fundraising, and vowed that she wouldn't enter the race unless she raised $2 million, but it was an uphill battle. Studying the fundraising documentation, she found that some of her supporters who gave $1,000 to men would then give her only $250. "I'd read this and think: do they think I get a discount?" Schroeder recalled that as the fall of 1987 came into view, a *Time* magazine poll had ranked her third in the Democratic field, "but when you looked at the polls, and how many people said they'd never vote for a woman, and then realized that a lot of people lied when they said yes, they would, I figured *no way this is going to happen; I'm gonna be third forever and third won't get me there*."

She decided to announce that she would not launch a formal campaign. And when she made her speech, she was so overcome by a series of emotions—gratitude for the people who'd supported and fought for her throughout a long hot summer, frustration with the system that made it so difficult to raise money and to target voters rather than delegates, and anger at the sexism—that she got choked up.

"You would have thought I'd had a nervous breakdown," recalled Schroeder of how the press reacted to her. "You'd have thought Kleenex was my corporate sponsor. I remember thinking, *What are they gonna put on my tombstone? 'She cried'?*" For a while Schroeder kept what she called "a crying file," a little list of all the male politicians who'd wept publicly that year. "Reagan would tear up every time he saw a flag," she remembered of the former president. Her file included references to Governor John Sununu, who cried as he was stepping down as governor of New Hampshire, and then–Vice President George H. W. Bush, who was a steady weeper. But the reaction to tears from those men was wholly different from what Schroeder got in response to hers.

Saturday Night Live mocked Schroeder in a skit in which actress Nora Dunn, as Schroeder, repeatedly burst into tears while moderating a debate. Later the *New York Times* described her as having dissolved "in a flood of tears." An editorial in one Vermont paper read, "What a devastating indictment of this girl's character." One *Washington Post* columnist wrote about how older women like Schroeder were setting the cause of young women back a century, calling it "crazy, reckless, for one of Congress's few women . . . to give ammunition to those who saw women as sugary little girls rather than serious people to be taken seriously."

Schroeder found this last argument the most frustrating. Recalling a man who *had* suffered politically after he wept in public, Edmund Muskie, whose tears effectively ended his bid for the presidency back in that crucial year 1972, she still wondered, thirty years later, "Why don't I remember anyone saying that he set *men* back?" Pat Schroeder remained a member of Congress, where she channeled her work-related frustrations into witty, sharp-tongued responses that didn't always fall merrily on the ears of her colleagues. Some of her witticisms became famous, like her dubbing Ronald Reagan "the Teflon president," because, like an egg cooking in a nonstick Teflon frying pan, scandal just slid off him. After the millionth time she was asked whether she would run for president "as a woman," she began to snap back "What choice do I have?" A *New York Times* story noting that Schroeder had been sworn into Congress with diapers in her purse also included reference to her most famous comeback, her response to being asked how she could be both a mother and a congresswoman: "I have a brain and a uterus, and I use both."

"That was obviously sharp, and I shouldn't have said it," Schroeder said to me in 2017, and has long noted—including in that same *Times* story—that "I don't think anyone likes a smart aleck." To me, she said, looking back, that a lot of her sharp humor was understood as aggression. She remembered being referred to by colleagues as "the wicked witch—or bitch—of the West." Schroeder recalled the unfairness of it all, noting that often her digs came in her own defense against sexist diminishment. "If a guy says something in his own defense," she said, "he's standing his ground. If you say it, you're just being petty or being thin-skinned. Women are just supposed to put up with it, suck it up, and move on."

The irony is that Schroeder was consciously using her wit and her cheery feminized persona—she famously drew smiling faces in the *P* in her signature and giggled a lot—to ease anxieties about her political ambitions, her willingness to speak out against her opponents, and her often confrontational style. When she was the most senior woman in Congress in 1990, the *New York Times* described Schroeder's "shrewd, even lethal political savvy," noting that "over the years she has helped bump not one, but two, chairmen off the House Armed Services

Committee." But she often cited advice from her father: "Never frown at your enemies. Smile—it scares the hell out of them."

Among the commands the antifeminist crusader Phyllis Schlafly issued *her* foot soldiers during her campaign against ratification of the ERA in the 1970s was that they should always, always smile; one of Schlafly's best-known books was titled *The Power of the Positive Woman*. But grinning positivity may disguise ambitious intent only in women fighting on the side of white patriarchy. After all, Schlafly defeated the ERA and was rarely pressed too hard on the hypocrisy of her message: As a powerful political woman who traveled the country, she was regularly telling other women that their calling was to stay at home. Meanwhile, despite all the smiley faces drawn by the left-leaning feminist Schroeder, her critics still saw in *her*, according to the *Times*, "a 'hard' look, a grin that is really a grimace, a nasal-voiced delivery through clenched jaws and eyes that disappear behind a squint. . . . The reality is that Schroeder is a driven politician who smiles too hard" and whose use of one-liners "often undercuts [her] seriousness."

The Year of the Woman

For women like Schroeder trying to push back against the tide of Reagan-era cuts to funding of government programs like schools and health care, there was no end of condescending criticism to which they were subject. In 1980, Patty Murray was a stay-at-home mom of two who became enraged after her state cut preschool funding. She put her kids in the car and drove to the state capitol to register her fury. "I was going around the hall and finding who I could talk to," Murray recalled to Jay Newton-Small, "and one state legislator said, 'That's a nice story, but you're just a mom in tennis shoes.'" Murray, further enflamed, went home and called the other moms in tennis shoes. "And they called the moms they knew—all were mad—and we were back at the state legislature." The women staged an uprising, ultimately succeeding in having the education cuts reversed, and Murray embarked on a career in electoral politics. She was among the historic group of four women to win seats in the US Senate in 1992; her campaign's tagline was "Just a mom in tennis shoes."

Murray's self-minimizing reputation has continued to disguise the anger that first prompted her entry into electoral politics. "[Patty's] not emotional," former Republican House Speaker Paul Ryan once said of Murray. "Some of these folks walk out of the room, and they huff and they puff. She's not like that."

Murray's 1992 victory for the US Senate seat was part of an electoral wave that swept Republicans out of the White House for the first time in twelve years and in which a record number of women were elected to office. It was called the Year of the Woman, and it also catapulted the first Black woman to the US Senate.

After Shirley Chisholm lost her bid for the presidency, she wrote in 1973, "What I hope most is that now there will be others who will feel themselves as capable of running for high political office as any wealthy, good-looking white male." Nearly twenty years later, Carol Moseley Braun ran for the US Senate from Illinois, driven in part by how she had felt, in 1991, when Clarence Thomas, a right-wing judge accused of sexual harassment, was nominated to the Supreme Court. "I was absolutely offended," Moseley Braun recalled to me in 2017. "No, that's too light a word. I was appalled."

The Thomas nomination "was such a complete repudiation of Thurgood Marshall's legacy," she said of the first Black Supreme Court justice, who was a staunch defender of civil rights. Marshall had served at the tail end of the Supreme Court term of Earl Warren, who, as chief justice, led the court to strike down legal segregation. "Marshall had been so important to the liberation of Black people, and this was turning the table over on everything the Warren court did. I had had a lifetime of possibilities because of the Warren Court; my husband was not Black, and our marriage would have been illegal but for the Warren Court; I had marched with Dr. King. The Clarence Thomas nomination was a repudiation of everything I had fought for or worked for and it would not stand was my attitude."

Moseley Braun was especially livid at the Illinois senator, Democrat Alan Dixon, who was planning to vote to confirm Thomas. She went to meet with him about it and came out even more angered about his stubbornness. "He was so obtuse about the whole thing, that the conversation lit a fire in my belly."

Moseley Braun, who'd served in the Illinois state legislature and in the US Attorney's office, challenged Dixon in a primary for the Senate seat in 1992 and beat him, becoming the first candidate to successfully topple a sitting senator in a primary in more than a decade. One of her campaign slogans was the unapologetically frank "We don't need another arrogant rich guy in the Senate." It worked. When she won her seat, she not only became the first Black woman ever elected to the United States Senate, but only the second African American senator elected since the post–Civil War

Reconstruction years. In the Senate, Moseley Braun became the first woman to sit on the Finance Committee, and she and Dianne Feinstein became the second and third women in history to join the Judiciary Committee, which gave her more say in evaluating nominees to the courts. "There was great anger," Moseley Braun said of the time. "There were people really, really mad and rightly so." And they used the tools of our democratic institutions—their votes—to make their voices heard.

No More Feminists

Despite the groundbreaking political races won during 1992's Year of the Woman, despite the election of Bill Clinton to the White House, accompanied by an enormously accomplished and trailblazing First Lady, Hillary Clinton, the political moment was not one of anger or stridency, insurgency or revolution. Who wanted to be a feminist? No one. Because during this ongoing backlash against Second Wave feminism, the term itself, the idea of public and politicized challenge to male dominance, was considered unattractively old, unhinged, ugly. To be sure, there were eruptions of fury, coming from people—often from women—who were waging battles against inequities, but they were less mainstream.

These years sometimes included violent rage in response to racism: In 1992, after four white cops were cleared by a mostly white jury in the brutal beating of African American taxi driver Rodney King in Los Angeles, the city erupted in fury. Angry protesters looted stores and set fires; sixty-three people died. At the time, the news media and local politicians were quick to describe the events as riots, throwing around the term "thugs."

But one Los Angeles Democratic representative saw something else in the riots: "There are those who would like for me . . . to tell people to go inside, to be peaceful, that they have to accept the verdict. I accept the responsibility of asking people not to endanger their lives. I am not asking people not to be angry," said first-term congresswoman Maxine Waters, who represented a large section of the South Central Los Angeles neighborhood where much of the unrest was unfolding. "I am angry and I have a right to that anger and the people out there have a right to that anger."

Waters spent days tending to her constituents, bringing food, water, and diapers to Angelenos living without gas or electricity; she also pushed to charge the police officers in civil court and objected to Mayor Tom Bradley's use of the word "riot" to describe events. Instead, she saw it as an uprising of the people who possessed little power against a system that was unjust and racist, framing their resentments as "an insurrection."

There were other moments of political protest, but much of the spirit of mass, brash, sustained political fury that had animated the 1960s and 1970s was muffled in the 1980s and stayed that way for decades. During the administration of George W. Bush from 2001 to 2009, despite policies that squeezed the middle class and cut programs on which working and poor people depended in order to deliver large tax cuts to the wealthy, political anger continued to be mostly muted. Code Pink was an exception, a grassroots organization launched by women in 2002 in opposition to the US-led Iraq War; Code Pink women then and now fearlessly and angrily confront lawmakers from all parties who stand in the way of peace. But after Barack Obama was elected president in 2008, political anger began to bubble over and break through this show of calm, in part driven by the angry voices of women, and in part by the voices who the press portrayed as angry, whether they were or not.

• 9 •

Who Can Be Angry

In the early 2000s, who was angry and how it was expressed made all the difference in how that anger was interpreted.

Michelle Robinson had grown up on Chicago's South Side, the daughter of a stay-at-home mother and a city employee. She graduated from Princeton and Harvard Law School, and met her future husband Barack Obama when she was assigned to professionally mentor him at a fancy Chicago law firm. During the years in which the couple lived in Chicago, when Barack worked as a community organizer and law professor, and Michelle left the law firm to work for the city and then for the University of Chicago, she was considered the star of the couple: the charming, charismatic, funny, dynamic one. Having grown up around Chicago's corrupt political machine, she was distrustful of politics and didn't want anything to do with them. But her husband did.

Then Barack Obama became the brightest star to streak across the American political landscape in a generation, and his wife fell under national scrutiny. Her impassioned speeches, her emotional honesty, her clear and informed view of American history, including her grim take on politics and her sharp sense of humor, all began, perplexingly, to work against her.

As her husband became a sensation in the US Senate, she was caught by a reporter rolling her eyes and commenting, "Maybe one day he will do something to warrant all this attention"; by the time he hit the presidential campaign trail two years later, she was still affectionately complaining about his failures to make the bed or put his socks in the laundry basket; she called him "snore-y and stinky" when he woke up in the morning and described him, memorably, as "a gifted man, but in the end, he's just a man." This quickly earned her the attention of the *New York Times* columnist Maureen Dowd, who worried that people heard Michelle as attacking his manhood and "emasculating" him, for "casting her husband . . . as an undisciplined child." The critical voice of a woman was presented as maternal scolding.

After her husband began to win primary elections and it seemed possible that he might win the Democratic nomination, Michelle gave a speech in which she said, "People in this country are ready for change and hungry for a different kind of politics. . . . For the first time in my adult life I am proud of my country because it feels like hope is finally making a comeback."

It was a positive, warm, forward-looking statement. But coming from the mouth of Michelle Obama, it was heard in some quarters as unpatriotic. The very act of mild critique—of a nation in which her great-great-great-grandmother had been enslaved, in which her husband was the first Black man ever to come close to being nominated for the presidency, in which she was being asked to sacrifice her job and independent identity to try to move into the White House, a building constructed by slave labor—was enough to confirm a popular vision of Michelle as a worryingly angry Black woman.

She appeared on the cover of the right-wing magazine *National Review*: mouth open as if in mid-yell, her eyes cutting menacingly toward the viewer, under the headline MRS. GRIEVANCE. The conservative columnist Michelle Malkin began referring to her as "Barack's Bitter Half." The Black conservative columnist Mychal Massie wrote that Michelle "portrays herself as just another angry black harridan who spits in the face of the nation that made her rich, famous, and prestigious."

As the novelist Chimamanda Ngozi Adichie would write of Michelle, "Because she said what she thought, and because she smiled only when she felt like smiling, and not constantly and vacuously, America's cheapest caricature was cast on her: the Angry Black Woman. Women, in general, are not permitted anger—but for black American women, there is an added expectation of interminable gratitude, the closer to groveling the better, as though their citizenship is a phenomenon that they cannot take for granted."

Medusa-Michelle memes exploded on the internet. The already incorrect description of Michelle as angry transformed into her being militant and became so intense that the campaign clearly began to feel the need to counter it.

By the time her husband was accepting the nomination in Denver, Michelle's public persona had been remade: She talked about clothes and pantyhose, not about politics or the nation, and not with any critical jokes about her spouse. At the convention, she was framed (accurately!) as a devoted wife and mother, a former little girl who'd loved the wholesome television family comedy *The Brady Bunch*, but as nothing else. In her own speech, she carefully expressed her love of country and gratitude for the chances it had afforded her. Michelle had been effectively muzzled, any negativity tamped down. She'd never actually expressed true anger on the trail, but the very act of having opened her mouth in a free and frank way had so quickly been heard as bitterness that her opinions and her open mouth, and anything that could be heard as frustration or complaint, had had to go.

Before she left the White House after eight years as First Lady, in an interview with Oprah Winfrey, Michelle said of that period, of being cast as "that angry Black woman," "You don't even *know* me, you know? . . . Where'd that come from?" More than a year later, Michelle—speaking at a gathering of Black women in Florida—spoke even more frankly to former White House advisor Valerie Jarrett of this process, explaining that early on, "I looked at one of my speeches and I saw that what was animation and passion to me, could easily be turned into sound bites of anger and aggression." At that point, she said, "I was like, *oh, this is a game*. It's a game. And what was I thinking? I thought this was real, but it was a game too. And I wasn't playing the game, I was just being passionate because I thought that's what people wanted . . . But they don't know what they really want. So I had to learn how to deliver"—and here she pasted a big smile on her face and offered a shake of her hair—"a *message*."

The negative reaction to the anger of Black women takes many forms. There's a defensiveness against it from white women and from men, a resistance to actually reckoning with the roots of Black female dissatisfaction. "We are told we are irrational, crazy, out-of-touch, entitled, disruptive, and not team players," writes Brittney Cooper in her exploration of Black feminist anger, *Eloquent Rage*. "Angry Black women are looked upon as entities to be contained, as inconvenient citizens who keep on talking about their rights while refusing to do their duty and smile at everyone."

Anger Right and Left

Perhaps the most politically effective strike during Obama's presidency came from the Republican right, with the Tea Party protests that began in 2009, soon after President Barack Obama took office. The economy had been crashing since before Obama's election during the Great Recession when, thanks in large part to President George W. Bush's failed economic policies, millions of people had lost their jobs, their homes, and their life savings. In response to Obama's plan to help some homeowners through the crisis, cable news reporter Rick Santelli angrily called on television for the "Tea Party" to object to Obama's spending plans. The reference was to the 1773 revolutionary protest of colonists who threw tea into Boston Harbor to object to being taxed by Britain, which had imposed taxes on colonists who had no representation in British Parliament.

In theory, the activism was in response to the far right's view that Barack Obama's administration was misusing taxpayer money, but the Tea Party was also driven by a wave of rage and racial resentment toward Barack Obama as the first Black president; no amount of Obama's nonconfrontational rhetoric could convince overwhelmingly white Tea Partiers he wasn't a threat to their status and supremacy.

Though the public face of the Tea Party protesters was that of furious white men—often dressed in colonial-era tricorn hats in their early gatherings—some polls indicated that the majority of Tea Party supporters were women. Its loudest early female voice belonged to former vice presidential candidate Sarah Palin, who in one address to activists called the movement "another revolution." In 2010, a number of Tea Party–affiliated female candidates ran for elective office; Palin, who'd cast herself as a pit-bullish hockey mom, dubbed them "Mama Grizzlies."

Somehow, as with Schlafly, these women voicing their anger and throwing around their political weight weren't caricatured as ugly hysterics in the popular media the way that feminists had been; instead they successfully cast themselves as patriotic moms on steroids, some bizarro-world embodiment of female empowerment, despite the fact (or, more precisely, *because* of the fact) that what they were advocating was a return to traditionalist roles for women and reduced government investment in nonwhite and non-wealthy people. Once they were elected to the United States Congress, their obsessive mission was to vote to take away the federal funding received by women's health care and family planning programs, to outlaw abortion, to punish Planned Parenthood, and to reduce government safety net programs such as food stamps, which give poor families money to buy food for hungry children.

"Conservative women have found their voices and are using them, actively and loudly," Tea Partier Rebecca Wales told *Politico* in 2010. Another Tea Partier, Darla Dawald, put it this way: "You know the old saying 'If Mama ain't happy, ain't nobody happy'? When legislation messes with Mama's kids and it affects her family, then Mama comes out fighting—and I don't mean in a violent way, of course."

As more moderate Republicans got knocked out of their seats in primary election contests by extremist right-wing Tea Party candidates, and those who remained in office shifted their positions further right, an angry protest in New York called Occupy Wall Street was drawing crowds of agitators from the other side. In the fall of 2011, in Zuccotti Park in downtown Manhattan, young people gathered to voice their fury at economic inequality; the widening gap between rich and poor; the tax breaks for big, wealthy companies; and the steady destruction of social welfare programs that provided support to people living in poverty, like medical care and help paying rent.

Similar to the Tea Party's impact on the Republican Party, Occupy Wall Street's impact on the American left and the Democratic Party was crucial and long-lasting; the movement helped to popularize the view of economic inequality that set 99 percent of Americans with moderate incomes or who were poor against the nation's richest 1 percent. It would help push the Democratic Party further left, boosting the profiles and fortunes of politicians including Elizabeth Warren, who was elected senator for Massachusetts in 2012, and Bernie Sanders, an independent who'd served in Congress for twenty-six years and would mount electrifying campaigns for the presidency in 2016 and again in 2020.

Many different types of people participated in Occupy—estimates varied, but reportedly around 40 percent of the protesters were women, and 37 percent identified as nonwhite. Yet it was nevertheless a movement dominated publicly by the voices and ideas of white men. There were enough allegations of assault and harassment of women at Zuccotti Park that, after several weeks, women-only tents were set up. Kanene Holder, an artist, activist, and Black woman who served as one of Occupy's spokespeople, told the *Guardian* that even within this left-wing, liberal, progressive space white men insisted on being in charge: "White males are used to speaking and running things. . . . You can't expect them to abdicate the power they have just because they are in this movement." Eventually, Occupy had to adopt special sessions in which women were encouraged to speak uninterrupted.

More than that, some of the righteously radical men who dominated Occupy were reportedly unwelcoming of internal feminist critique. As one activist, Ren Jender, wrote, "I was angry with the greater number of people who hadn't confronted the misogyny." Occupy was a reminder to many who agreed with its principles that the left was no more free of gender hierarchies and power abuses than the rest of the country.

Then, in 2012, Trayvon Martin, a seventeen-year-old Black boy was shot and killed by George Zimmerman. A year later, after a jury found Zimmerman not guilty of murder, the longtime progressive activist Alicia Garza wrote a note on Facebook that concluded with the sentences, "Black people, I love you. I love us. We matter. Our lives matter." The artist and activist Patrisse Khan-Cullors appended a hashtag to it, #BlackLivesMatter; the writer and community organizer Ayọ Tometi (known as Opal Tometi at the time) helped to push the message out over social media.

A movement—born of grief, horror, and unleashed fury at the persistent killing of African Americans by the state, by the police—was born. And while it, like Occupy and the Tea Party, was purposefully nonhierarchical in its internal structure, it had been founded by women, and many of the most prominent voices of the movement belonged to women, including Brittany Packnett, Johnetta Elzie, Nekima Levy Armstrong (then Nekima Levy-Pounds), and Elle Moxley (then Elle Hearns). Khan-Cullors later wrote of how Black liberation movements of the past had been led largely by straight men, "leaving women, who are often queer or transgender, either out of the movement or in the background to move the work forward with little or no recognition. As younger organizers, we recognized a need to center the leadership of women."

Black Lives Matter increased national awareness of racist policing practices that had remained largely invisible, especially to white eyes, but which millions of Americans now understand to be a systemic reality, built into how police officers are trained and how the justice system treats Black people. The movement, which spread across the country and the world, staged days of protest in Ferguson, Missouri, after the police killing of Michael Brown; activists pioneered a new age of public demonstration, staging "die-ins," in which protesters lay on the ground in recognition of African Americans gunned down in the streets. In 2015, in the wake of the mass killing of Black churchgoers by a white man in Charleston, activist Bree Newsome scaled the flagpole at the South Carolina state house, removing the

Confederate flag that had long hung there in commemoration of the slave-holding tradition of the Southern state when slavery was still legal more than a century earlier. Her act provoked a wave of removal of statues of Confederate leaders throughout the South.

Around the same time there was growing anger about and awareness of environmental injustice and the quashing of the rights of indigenous people bubbling out of South Dakota. In 2015, the Standing Rock Sioux Tribe passed a resolution in opposition to the Dakota Access Pipeline, a crude-oil pipeline from North Dakota to Illinois that threatened the safety of the clean water on which the Standing Rock Indian Reservation depended. In April of the following year, LaDonna Brave Bull Allard formed the Sacred Stone Camp, which hosted hundreds of activists every day to try to stop the building of the pipeline; Black Lives Matter sent a delegation to join the protests in solidarity.

Young people in particular were leaders in the struggle. When she was just twelve years old, Tokata Iron Eyes, a member of the Standing Rock Sioux Tribe, became an outspoken "water protector." Described by the writer Naomi Klein as "a fiercely grounded yet playful water-warrior," Iron Eyes later detailed her understanding of how the struggles at Standing Rock were linked to other social justice movements. In 2020 she told the writer Tess Thomas, "In a lot of ways, we're fighting for the same things that we knew about and that we knew were completely preventable 200 years ago. Like reckless killing of Black and Brown bodies, that's still happening. Displacement of peoples from their homelands, still happening. The climate crisis, not living in a way that is in tune with the Earth's natural systems and ways of being, these are all things that we 100% knew about and knew that they were bad, knew that they were catastrophically violent and still did."

In the years leading up to the 2016 presidential election, there was a building, public rage—rage that had an impact on politics, on public spaces, on civic structures that shape how we engage with one another politically. In many ways, the speed and breadth of this engagement were fueled by technological innovations that changed the ways we consumed news and interacted with one another, in particular the inventions of smartphones and the spread of social media. The first iPhone was released in 2007, within just a few years of the creation of Facebook, Twitter, and other social media companies. Smartphones put the world in our pockets, ensuring we could stay up-to-date and entertained and in touch no matter where we were, at all times of the day and night. Social media sites found ways to keep us hooked: through algorithms that feed us personally customized and curated content that stokes our outrage, click by click. Our phones get to know us: our politics and our preferences, our "likes," and even the number of milliseconds we spend hovering over a story or a post or an item of clothing. The companies use all that data to keep our eyeballs glued to the screen, and usually that's done by pushing content that infuriates or terrifies us.

There were advantages to social media and smartphones too. People could feel less isolated and more easily connect with others who shared their beliefs. This made political organizing more immediate, more responsive, and more inclusive. Voicing an opinion was no longer limited to a select few with book contracts or jobs in television. Women were finding new ways to broadcast their powerful, desperately felt anger to the nation. And, at least on the left, they were doing it in a way that specifically challenged patriarchal, male-dominated histories of movement-building. But in mainstream feminism, there was a different spirit. Hot fury—expressed through public acts of protest, mass movements to the streets, or defiant curses yelled loudly at the powerful—was simply not the main mode of feminist expression. And it's not that feminism itself was dying.

· 10 ·

Feminist Cool

What used to be called "the women's movement" found energetic new life in the media in the first decades of the twenty-first century. After years of backlash, feminist journalists and bloggers revived a conversation about gender, and many of us who participated in that conversation were angry—angry about sexism and racism and economic inequality, and how all these injustices were woven together. But, perhaps anxious to set ourselves apart from the spitting-mad, crocodile-mask-wearing feminists of the past, many contemporary feminists (including me) worked to make the expression of our frustrations sound agreeable, relatable, and inviting to others, including to the very men who might have a hand in oppressing us.

Young feminists traded in jokey signifiers of man-hating: mugs and T-shirts reading I BATHE IN MALE TEARS. The hashtag #banmen conveyed frustration with bad men in a way that mocked the absurd notion that feminists hated *all* men. And while plenty of men's rights activists did not see these sentiments as funny or ironic, the exaggerations radiated reassurance: that a truly abrasive challenge to patriarchy wasn't a real political threat, rather the stuff of screen-printed T-shirt punch lines. New, mainstream feminism was funny, hip . . . and kind of cool.

And, not for nothing, it worked! In the years leading up to 2016, feminism was becoming a bit trendy. There were all-women reboots of *Ghostbusters* and female Jedis in *Star Wars* and powerful female leads all over television whose stories exposed the limitations still put on women by the patriarchy. But a lot of the critique was gentle, not vulgar, not *animal*. Not angry.

In 2013, Facebook mogul Sheryl Sandberg published *Lean In*, a book looking at the disadvantages still faced by women in the workplace; it focused largely on individual behavioral strategies to get around inequities, earning sharp, fair criticism for not focusing more on systemic overhaul of the structures—rules and ingrained attitudes and corporate interests—that kept women from fully flourishing in the workplace. This incomplete but unapologetic expression of feminist complaint, from someone who had risen within the system, became a massive bestseller.

The next year, Beyoncé performed at the MTV Video Music Awards, backed up by a recording of Chimamanda Ngozi Adichie's TED Talk "We Should All Be Feminists": "We teach girls to shrink themselves, to make themselves smaller. We say to girls 'You can have ambition, but not too much. You should aim to be successful, but not too successful. Otherwise, you will threaten the man.'" Then up came a giant bright sign, FEMINIST, and Beyoncé, glittering like a disco ball, stood in front of it.

It was pop culture, packaged and polished to a high gloss. But it was also a feminist assertion delivered by a woman of color, citing another woman of color, a crucial but powerful correction to the ways in which media had historically (and falsely) presented the project of women's liberation as having been led by white women. Here was a woman who had built up enough power—had become, arguably, the most powerful person in pop music at the time—to create her own story: She was not left at the margins to yell at reporters about what they were getting wrong or ignoring. Beyoncé had certainly made compromises with power structures, but she also seemed to have delivered on the promise of what a new, less furious, less confrontational approach to feminism could achieve: broad, attractive appeal.

And that was it, wasn't it? The loud, angry battles waged by earlier generations of women had produced some dramatic results. An admittedly small number of women who had gained unprecedented power—within colleges and graduate schools, in business, in entertainment, in media, in politics—had begun to enjoy opportunity and power that had historically been denied. And if those women wanted to move forward, they couldn't afford to behave in the confrontational, angry ways that had marked a past approach to a fight for something closer to actual equality. Because that challenge, that fury, would designate them as outsiders, as marginal. To have climbed within the system was to agree not to tear it down, not to remind America too aggressively of its gender and racial inequities or distract from the cheery view of progress and empowerment.

I have lived some form of this myself: I am a white woman who has been angry in my life and my work, occasionally on my own behalf but more often about politics, about inequity and the grotesque unfairness of the world, this country, how it was built, and who it still excludes and systematically diminishes. Some of that rage has become the driving force of my professional life. For twenty years I have written, as a journalist, about women in media and politics and entertainment from a feminist perspective; that work itself has been rooted in anger, and in turn often strengthened by critics who got mad at me, and forced me to reconsider my perspective and think differently and more rigorously about race and class and sexuality and identity and opportunity. I value my own rage and the rage of others, especially of women.

But I also live in the world. I have, for years, made the rage that guided my work easy to swallow. I'd absorbed the message that open anger was needlessly overdramatic and unattractive—that it would be too much, really—and I had worked to accommodate these assumptions, softening my fury in my writing. As thoughtful as I tried to be about gender, racial, and economic inequality, I'd nevertheless, on some level, swallowed the myth that circumstances were no longer so severe that they called for, or could be effectively addressed by, livid public display. I had soaked in the warning that women who talked too loudly and too aggressively were considered immensely unappealing by the men whose opinions still shaped the world. That to be openly angry was a bad idea. That even when things were bad, a friendlier approach was preferable, for strategic, aesthetic, and moral reasons.

So in the years in which I started to write from a directly feminist perspective, I made sure that I was funny! And playful, cheeky, ironic, knowing! I worked to make it clear that I am a fun person who enjoys friends, fun, laughter. I took great care to be nice and respectful to opposing viewpoints. To full-throatedly express my ire would have been alienating, strategically foolish. I watched as my peers made similar choices. But all the good humor and in-jokes can't cover for the reality of wrath, the thing that makes you want to hit a wall or smash a glass or throw something, the electric impulse that occasionally streaks across our brains, making reason fuzz out, and our insides light up like firecrackers. Many of us who may have covered our fury in humor have occasionally found ourselves exploding.

In 2014, I was writing a semi-regular column for the *New Republic*. One day, I was tired. I was pregnant. I was mad at my workplace for a variety of reasons having to do with my pregnancy and my economic status in relation to my gender. I read some things in other publications that infuriated me: dismissive and demeaning articles about women's looks and about sexual assault. This was the summer when a mother had been arrested for letting her nine-year-old play alone while she worked her McDonald's shift; the Supreme Court had decided that corporations could choose not to provide birth control for their employees based on religious belief, and also that abortion clinic protesters were free to get close up and scream into the faces of women seeking reproductive health care.

The column I wrote, quickly, was its own reflection on my willingness to get mad in public: In it, I expressed my yearning for a world in which women's worth was no longer measurable on scales fashioned by men, be they cultural, legal, legislative . . . or expressive. For a moment, I felt completely done with—temporarily unable to tolerate—the male-determined metrics of female acceptability, and in my exhausted ire, I did something that I had previously understood to be unacceptable: I wrote out of acidic and untempered anger. Perhaps for the first time in my writing life, I myself did not care if readers liked that I was mad.

To my surprise, that column quickly became the most popular I'd ever written; it went viral; my friend from an evangelical Midwestern community told me that her religious childhood friends were posting it on their Facebook pages. There had been something in my eruption that had worked, communicatively.

Bursts like this, in this era, were rare blips, but they stood out. Like in 2014, when Congress failed to pass the Paycheck Fairness Act, which would have added protections to the Equal Pay Act and better ensured equal pay for women, especially women of color, Maryland Senator Barbara Mikulski gave a speech on the Senate floor. "I'll tell you what I'm tired of hearing: that somehow or another we're too emotional when we talk," Mikulski thundered. "Well, I am emotional . . . It brings tears to my eyes, to know how women every single day are working so hard and are getting paid less. It makes me emotional to hear that. Then when I hear all of these phony reasons, some are mean and some are meaningless, I do get emotional. I get angry. I get outraged. I get volcanic."

Mostly, though, no one wanted to get too close to these small explosions; they were still too hot to touch, and there was still too much to be gained by going along with things as they had always been. Anyone who wants power within a white male power structure has been asked to hush anything that sounds like fury, to reassure that they come in cooperative peace and are not looking to punish those who have oppressed or subjugated them. Women signaling wrath—by cursing, organizing, marching, yelling, threatening revenge—would have been marked as unstable forces, exactly what couldn't happen going into a 2016 election in which there seemed for the first time in American history to be a chance that the country would elect a woman and protect the legacy of the nation's first Black president.

As Hillary Clinton geared up in 2015 to run for the presidency the following year, the stakes were far too high for the kind of anger that had been so openly and defiantly expressed by the activists—in suffrage, abolition of slavery, civil rights, feminism—whose achievements had, ironically, made her candidacy possible. Female power was visible at the Video Music Awards; it was the chief operating officer of Facebook. It was in the *Ghostbusters* reboot and a slick, funny feminist media, and the inevitable presidential candidate. What was there to complain about?

• 11 •

What Is Likable About That?

The first time I entered a voting booth I was nine years old. It was 1984, and my parents had brought me with them so that I could pull the lever for the first woman ever to run on a major party presidential ticket. I remember walking proudly with my father and mother and younger brother into the suburban Philadelphia firehouse five blocks from the house in which I grew up, where the poll watchers knew my parents by name because they were two of the very few registered Democrats in our district.

I remember the weight of the curtain closing behind me and my father lifting me up to turn the black lever to make the *X* appear next to Walter Mondale's and Geraldine Ferraro's names. Ferraro was the first ever woman to be nominated for vice president of the United States. I remember my dad putting me back down so that he could turn the buttons for the other Democrats, and then telling me to pull the rubber-covered metal bar back as hard as I could, until the machine made a clanging noise that meant my vote had been counted.

When we left the fire station, my brother and I climbed into the back seat of our car, and my mother turned to make sure our seat belts were fastened; my father looked at us through the rearview mirror. "I hope that someday you'll have the chance to vote for a woman at the top of a presidential ticket," he said before starting the car and driving us home.

Almost twenty-four years later, I had that chance when Hillary Clinton first ran for president in 2008. After serving eight years as First Lady in Bill Clinton's White House, in 2000 she became the first woman elected to the US Senate from New York state. Back then there was plenty of commentary about her voice and her aggressive, ambitious demeanor, which often got confused with each other. Her tone was understood on many levels to sound inherently villainous: Whether it was when she laughed—routinely referred to in the press as her "cackle"—or when she spoke loudly, it was heard to match what was largely believed to be her threatening ambition. Back then, *Washington Post* reporter Joel Achenbach fantasized about the good old days of the brank's bridle, writing that Clinton "needs a radio-controlled shock collar so that aides can zap her when she starts to get screechy."

In 2008, the reaction to Clinton was in part about the sheer novelty of hearing a woman's voice on a presidential campaign trail, and her volume and pitch stood out especially against that of her opponent for the Democratic nomination Barack Obama, who, for reasons relating to his own historic identity and firstness, could not afford to raise *his* voice in anger, and whose calm tone and eloquence proved a stark contrast to Clinton's. After Obama won, Clinton served successfully as his secretary of state, and her popularity rose, but she would continue to be caricatured as threatening and angry.

The 2016 election was a different ball game. From the start, the theme of the presidential race *was* anger: Bernie Sanders, who ran against Clinton in the Democratic primary, was angry. Donald Trump, running in the Republican primary, was angry, telling CNN, "I am angry. . . . As far as I'm concerned, anger is okay. Anger and energy is what this country needs." Ten days later, Sanders took a similar approach, responding to Bill Clinton's description of him as angry. "You know what? It's true. I am angry. And the American people are angry." Four days later, Clinton herself got into the act. "A lot of people are not only worried and frustrated," she said. "They're angry. . . . I'm angry too."

But somehow Clinton couldn't persuade people that she was furious in the same way, perhaps in part because she couldn't quite get the tone of her voice right. A *Washington Post* write-up that included coverage of that speech opened with a description of how Clinton's voice "thundered through a bowling alley . . . then turned soft and thoughtful." The rest of the piece included two descriptions of Clinton as "shouting" and ended with a quote from one of Clinton's supporters, who said, "Bernie Sanders has an ability to connect in a charismatic way. It's that magnetism that she's not inherently able to transmit." How could a candidate whose firm expressions of anger were understood only as fake and inauthentic *also* be heard by so many people, at the very same time, as constantly yelling at them?

After her first debate with Sanders, the *New York Times* evaluated the Vermont senator—whose everyday communication style involves finger-pointing, raised tones, and vigorous head-shaking—as having "kept his cool," while claiming that Clinton "appear[ed] tense and even angry at times" and wondered if her "ferocity" wasn't "risky, given that many voters . . . already have an unfavorable opinion of her." The famed journalist Bob Woodward suggested that Clinton's challenges originated with her "style and delivery . . . she shouts. There is something unrelaxed about the way she's communicating." On his radio show, after playing a clip of Clinton talking loudly—yes, angrily!—about standing up to the gun lobby that represents gun manufacturers and has flooded this country with more guns than there are people, the right-wing host Sean Hannity asked, "What is likable about that? . . . Angry, bitter, screaming?"

It was a perfect, and perfectly maddening, circle of entrapment: a candidate who yelled too much, but who didn't express anger enough, and when she tried to express anger better, was presumed to be faking it. Edie Abraham-Macht, a friend of mine who was sixteen years old during the 2016 race, summed up the frustrating impossibility of Clinton's dilemma: "Everything that a woman says in a political context is subject to additional layers of screening. And the biggest one of those is: Is there emotion involved? And I just think emotion is involved in everything. It's involved in decision-making. It's involved in politics."

The irony was that Clinton's economic proposals as a candidate for president were directly targeted at helping many of the populations that were angriest, groups that her opponents were successfully wooing. Clinton had policies to help people afford childcare and to create more economic stability for caregivers, on addressing racial and economic inequality, and supporting women's rights to make their own decisions about their reproductive health. But she was widely understood to be bad at talking about these issues in a persuasive way, and part of that badness surely did stem from her own weaknesses as a communicator. But those shortcomings might well have been exaggerated by all the ways that Clinton—and lots of public-speaking women who came before her—had been discouraged from talking loudly or too aggressively, leaving her nervous and hesitant about getting too passionate, too enflamed, too screechy or shrill or emotional or any of the other ways America hears women's voices raised in feeling. She had to walk a very thin communicative tightrope, often sounding boring and robotic, wholly unable to convey her interest in the frustrations of voters.

That the forceful expression of fury might not just be okay from (white) men but might in fact actually work to their benefit, while at the same time working *against* their female peers and competitors, is backed up by some emerging research. The psychology professor Lisa Feldman Barrett has described in the *New York Times* a study in which her research team showed people photographs of men and women making facial expressions. They found that their subjects were more likely to assume that whatever was causing a woman's emotion was something internal, whereas whatever was provoking a man's response was something external, or as she put it, "She's a bitch, but he's just having a bad day."

It's a problem that John Neffinger, a political advisor who's been coaching candidates for years, and who wrote a series of memos to Clinton during the presidential race, trying to help her balance the ways in which she expressed herself, has been wrestling with. He and fellow researchers reviewed studies on two general criteria in how the public evaluates candidates: strength and warmth. Going in, he explained, male candidates are presumed to have strength—a category imaginatively tied to skill, authority, capability, and economic power; and female candidates are assumed to possess warmth—which in political terms is meant to convey fellow feeling, fun, friendliness, and also the sense that a candidate really cares about the people they want to represent.

"When somebody manages to project a lot of strength and a lot of warmth, we say they're charismatic and magnetic, we want to be *with* that person, we want to *be* that person," said Neffinger. Those who read as having more strength than warmth are viewed as "fearsome" and those with more warmth than strength as "adorable." The question of how these qualities are valued in politicians is as old as the argument by the sixteenth-century philosopher Niccolo Machiavelli that it is better to be feared than loved, though best to be both. According to Neffinger, "It's really hard to find candidates who combine the two." Male candidates *can* theoretically squeak by as fearsome, especially in times of national crisis, when authoritarian male figures are generously viewed as protectors. They can't be wholly adorable, precisely because that means they've been feminized and are therefore taken less seriously.

For women, both options are toxic: To be fearsome is to be vilified as unnatural and monstrous. To be adorable is to be unserious and incompetent. The strategic problem for women is that the work to balance both poles is delicate and hazardous: As it turns out, for men, a little warmth goes a long way. For women, a little strength goes way too far.

Bernie Sanders, a scruffy grump whose style was to yell righteously but repetitively at his audiences about inequality, was able to ooze charm simply by smiling at a small bird that landed on his podium during a speech. But when a woman, said Neffinger, "asserts herself in some fashion having to do with strength, she quickly slides out of the warmth category. She becomes perceived as a threat to the social order. Guys can be a little nice, without throwing out their strength. But women cannot add a little strength without losing warmth."

Those were the dynamics facing Hillary Clinton as she competed against two men who were trading on their strength—their anger—as a major selling point to the American public. To compete with them in this way would be to invite additional anxiety about the ways in which she was already upsetting the order of things simply by running against these men for the highest office in the land. And no one on her team was naive about what kind of impact these conditions had on her range of expression.

As her lead speechwriter, Dan Schwerin, told me in 2017, "There's a reason why male candidates can shout and are called passionate, and if a woman candidate raises her voice to whip up a crowd, she's screeching and yelling." Because his boss understood this, Schwerin said, she kept her voice down, but then it seemed as if she didn't care as much as her opponents did: "She's controlled, she doesn't rant and rave, she's careful. And then that's read as inauthentic; it means that she doesn't understand how upset people are, or the pain people are in, because she's not angry the way those guys are angry. So she must be okay with the status quo because she's not angry."

Clinton herself addressed her frustration with this seemingly unsolvable equation in her campaign memoir *What Happened*, barely able to contain her simmering scorn for the impossibility of the dynamics facing her as a candidate. "I've tried to adjust," she wrote. "After hearing repeatedly that some people didn't like my voice, I enlisted the help of a linguistic expert," who told her to focus on deep breathing and positivity. Clinton is drily smoldering as she explains how she was pushed to such *un*natural lengths to maintain the illusion of a naturally cheery femininity: "That way, when the crowd got energized and started shouting—as crowds at rallies tend to do—I could resist doing the normal thing, which is to shout back." Clinton told the linguistic expert that she'd try her best to comply. "But out of curiosity, can you give me an example of a woman in public life who has pulled this off successfully—who has met the energy of a crowd while keeping her voice soft and low?"

The linguistic expert could not.

Any hint of truly angry, truly challenging feminist resentment behind a political movement would get criticized as fake. Authentic expressions of resistance—marches, hunger strikes, demonstrations, sit-ins—had been useful for getting attention, banging down doors, forcing women's way in. But the public antics and outpourings of vivid fury at an unequal system that had been useful in eras when women were so far from the inside would work against those who'd *gotten* inside, making them look and sound like outsiders once more.

The Grand Illusion

Of course women weren't *really* inside. And you could tell because the ones who looked to be had actually walked into the most ingenious trap of all: the one in which their insider status, the illusion of their assured claim to political power, gained after centuries of exclusion, would be the very thing that worked to disqualify them.

When Hillary Clinton began her second campaign for the presidency, not only had we not elected a single woman president in 226 years of presidential history, we had not elected a single woman *vice* president. Presidential candidates must first win enough primary races within their parties to be nominated to run against the candidate of the opposite party in any November general election, and despite the more than two hundred women who had thrown their hats in, the country had never managed even to make a woman a major party *nominee* for the presidency. Congress was still only 19 percent female and had only ever elected one Black woman to the Senate. And all these representational gaps existed in a country in which women were losing rights over their bodies and health care choices, and their wages and economic stability were under new attacks from a right-wing political agenda.

Yet the climate was one in which furious displays of anger on behalf of women's equality had been replaced by some milder forms of agitation coming from the few who *had* worked their way to power, spreading the myth that centuries of gender and racial discrimination were over, that things were pretty much even, that those who had been barred from power historically now possessed an equal share of it.

The fantasy that racism and sexism were stages through which the country had successfully passed, leaving new kinds of people, like President Barack Obama and "inevitable" next president Hillary Clinton, in charge, had unleashed another kind of rage, that of those *already* on the inside: the greedy anger of white American men who had, over centuries, enjoyed a lopsided share of political, economic, social, and gender power, and who were explosively furious at the prospect that others—women, people of color—were grabbing shares away from them.

The political profile of Donald Trump was built on his racist "birther" campaign, his public claims that Barack Obama's presidency had always been illegitimate because, Trump falsely asserted, Obama was not born in the United States. Trump's campaign kicked off with vile statements and lies about Mexican immigrants and promises to build walls and make laws to keep foreign intruders out. Trump's scorn for women was on prominent display from the start: He called them pigs, dogs, evaluated them on scales of one to ten, had run demeaning beauty pageants, been accused by his first wife of rape, and bragged of never having changed a diaper. He had told a magazine that women should be treated like dirt, but he used more vulgar wording.

Because of the national illusion that we as a country were too culturally advanced for this kind of backward white patriarchal expression, we were regularly assured by political experts that Trump's candidacy would never get off the ground, that these kinds of rants of racist and sexist resentment and dismissal would make him ineligible for the presidency.

But not only did Trump seem to surge ahead in *spite* of his hatred and dismissal of nonwhite non-men, his supporters seemed to love him *because* of it. His rallies were boisterous and furious events, stadium-sized yell-ins, with supporters offering Nazi salutes and wearing the symbols of white nationalists who believed that white people were superior and should be in control of society. Trump encouraged angry violence in his crowds, and his supporters acted like furious protesters themselves, screaming insults and curses at anyone they imagined to be challenging their authority.

And then there was the fury with which Trump supporters treated Hillary Clinton: Effigies of the candidate in prison uniforms and coffins were carried at Fourth of July parades in the summer of 2016; Trump's crowds were energized by their hatred, screaming profane insults toward her and bristling with threats of violence. At a North Carolina rally, Trump told his supporters that Clinton wanted to take away their guns, and, nudging them toward bloodshed, hinted at Clinton's assassination. More direct was his advisor on veterans affairs, a state representative from New Hampshire named Al Baldasaro, who said in a radio interview that Clinton "should be put in the firing line and shot for treason."

The extreme hatred of Clinton was sometimes only slightly more hushed on the left, in part because of the sticky truth of her position: She *did* have power, she was one of the exceptional women to have risen within a white patriarchal capitalist system that hadn't been built for her, and she'd risen in part by participating in it. Other women who'd attempted runs for the presidency, from Shirley Chisholm in 1972 to Patricia Schroeder in 1987, had been stopped by their outsider status or their inability to raise money or gain enough serious support from the powerful men who ran their party. Clinton had been hell-bent on overcoming these hurdles, but in doing so, had offered her opponents on the left the ammunition to undercut and undermine the historic nature of her candidacy.

Clinton's closeness with the power structure encouraged many on the left to support her primary opponent, the genuinely left-wing Democratic Socialist senator from Vermont, Bernie Sanders, a man who had long retained his independence from the Democratic Party. The Sanders campaign turned into its own kind of upbeat social movement. But some of the left's loathing for Clinton, and for her supporters, could often seem as though it were about more than simple policy differences or distrust of the establishment. It often was expressed through sexist remarks and memes. Edie Abraham-Macht, who was in tenth grade during the 2016 primary, told me years later that she remembered "being so annoyed at the Bernie Bro Boys in my grade, because I feel like there's lots of valid reasons for Bernie, but they, I felt like, were just doing it out of a sexist place." On both the right and the left, a kind of foul-mouthed, performative anger was in 2016 being directed at the woman who had come closer to the presidency than any other before her.

We're Not Cheerful Anymore

At the same time, as the reality that Donald Trump was going to be the Republican nominee for president set in, revelations of his vile behavior toward women became better known. Trump was open in his view of women's bodies and their functions as grotesque: He called Clinton's trip to the bathroom during a debate "disgusting," made a comment about debate moderator Megyn Kelly having "blood coming out of her wherever," and had once told a lawyer who'd had to take a break to pump breast milk during a meeting, "You're disgusting." It was perfectly clear that when he promised to "Make America Great Again," part of what Donald Trump was promising was a return to a retro version of white masculinity, and all the cruelty and hatred toward women that came along with it.

That he was the candidate felt absurd, backward, in the era we were assured no longer required a robust feminism. The idea that the nation had moved beyond macho white attitudes about who could lay claim to political power had always been a fable, one that had worked to discourage the disruptive fury that might otherwise have had more power to beat back Trump before his rise.

When, a month before the election, it was revealed that Donald Trump had been caught on a recording joking about women with Billy Bush on the TV show *Access Hollywood* about how "when you're a star, they let you do it. You can do anything . . . grab 'em by" their private parts, people got mad. Women got mad. The night that the *Access Hollywood* recording was made public, a Canadian author, Kelly Oxford, tweeted, "Women: tweet me your first assaults. They aren't just stats. I'll go first." She wrote that an old man on a bus once groped her when she was just twelve years old. In response came more than twenty million tweets and visits to her Twitter page, many posting under the hashtag #notokay to signify stories of unwanted sexual contact, many women recalling incidents from when they were children or teens.

The next week, women began to come forward with stories about how Trump himself had kissed or groped them against their will. "We accepted it for years," one of the women, Jessica Leeds, told the *New York Times*. "We were taught it was our fault." But hearing Trump deny on television, in response to the *Access Hollywood* recording, that he had ever grabbed a woman against her will, Leeds said, "I wanted to punch the screen."

Michelle Obama—the nation's First Lady, who had been caricatured during her husband's 2008 campaign as an angry Black woman and had worked relentlessly to battle that perception—roared to furious life, making a remarkable speech, in which she called out the "hurtful, hateful language about women" that Trump had been using on the campaign trail; she described how the flood of stories from women about abuse and harassment had "shaken me to my core in a way that I couldn't have predicted." It was an important speech, in part because it had been Mrs. Obama who that summer had told Democrats, "When they go low, we go high." The Republicans might behave in sexist and racist ways, but Democrats should behave with the confidence that morality would surely win the day.

Now Obama was mad. She called out the press for its inattention to women's anger, those who were "treating this as just another day's headline, as if our outrage is overblown or unwarranted." Powerfully, Michelle Obama argued that there was something to *do* with this outrage, urging all the women out there who were angry to take action. "While our mothers and grandmothers were often powerless to change their circumstances, today, we as women have all the power we need to determine the outcome of this election. We have knowledge. We have a voice. We have a vote."

Many women took Obama's words to heart. We were furious, but many were also optimistic that Clinton's victory was assured. This certainty, that Clinton had already won the presidency, was part of what may have prompted so many white people, including white women, to vote against the rise of women, especially against *the* woman who'd been so effectively vilified on both the left and the right. In treating her as though she had already beaten him, and not like the single tool on the table with which the nation might stop this monstrous, racist patriarch, we talked ourselves out of the outrage we should have been mustering. We didn't have to be angry on *behalf* of Hillary Clinton, this seductive song went. If anything, we should be angry *at* her, for not having done enough for us with the power we imagined she had.

Americans who might have exerted more energy to oppose Trump or support Clinton—especially white women—were driven to *in*action by the assurance that sexism and racism were things of the past, and that to work themselves up about either would look silly, would be unnecessary effort on behalf of an imperfect candidate (pro tip for your political future: There is no such thing as a perfect candidate). And of course, many other Americans—including white women—were moved to support Trump for essentially the same reason: what they heard as the *threat* that white patriarchy had lost its grip.

Which is why Donald Trump kept doubling down on his sexist language and threats. To fight her, and her predecessor—another history-making challenge to white masculinity—the Republican Party had chosen a figure who embodied every one of the strains of oppression and disrespect that had historically worked to keep women and nonwhite men away from the presidency and to deny them equal access to political power.

It worked. He won.

PART THREE
Resistance

• 12 •

The Winter of Our Discontent

The first election of Donald Trump over Hillary Clinton for the presidency of the United States in 2016 may have felt like a stinging, agonizing shock to many of us who lived through it. But in the context of American history, it should have been wholly unsurprising. In the wake of a challenge to white supremacy, in the form of two Obama administrations, racism won. Over the threat of a potential female leader, brutal masculinity won. For older women, the story was familiar: the sexist, egotistical, lying, hypocritical bigot who gets the big job over the woman, even when he's less qualified. This was not extraordinary; this was just another Tuesday in America.

We'd allowed ourselves to be taken in by the lie, by the illusion that we had come further than we had, and in so doing, we'd given up our right to be furious. We'd permitted those who *had* expressed anger or passion on behalf of Clinton to become the punch lines, and not the prophets. In the wake of her loss, there was no longer an immediate tool at hand—no candidate who could beat this man and his administration of men who would be revealed as wife-beaters and harassers and corrupt con artists and racists. It would be years before an election would provide an opportunity to replace or tame him, and now the anger poured out in ways that were unexpected even by the women expressing it.

The night after the election, Teresa Shook, a retired lawyer and grandmother in Hawaii, feeling shocked and shattered, made a Facebook page proposing a march on Washington set for the day after Trump's inauguration. By the time she woke up the next morning, she had ten thousand replies; meanwhile, New York fashion designer Bob Bland had had the same idea. It wasn't a fluid organizational process, but within a couple of weeks, organizers from other movements had taken over the event. Tamika Mallory, a gun-control advocate; Carmen Perez, who had worked on behalf of criminal justice reform; and Linda Sarsour, a Muslim rights activist who'd been active on Bernie Sanders's campaign, all joined Bob Bland to organize the millions who would show up not just in Washington, but in cities around the country and the world—including in Antarctica. Women were amassing—not always as smoothly or peaceably as we might have wished—and getting into some rough sort of formation.

The Women's March on January 21, 2017, was at the time the biggest one-day political protest in this country's history, and it was staged by angry women. Here was an inauguration protest that spanned all fifty states, led by a young, multiracial coalition of women hoping to pull a new version of the feminist movement into the future. "I've never felt as un-conflicted about what was right as I did then," said teenage participant Edie Abraham-Macht. It was groundbreaking, and they were (imperfectly but insistently) also pushing leftist progressive priorities—including civil rights, reproductive rights, disability rights, immigrant rights, workers' rights, economic equality, and environmental justice—all within a feminist framework, an intersectional feminism that recognized that women's oppression has long been tangled up in various other forms of oppression.

A switch had flipped: Marchers told reporters that they were thinking of running for office, and if they were not thinking of running for office themselves, they were looking at their local- and state-level candidates with an eye toward volunteering, organizing, and donating; they described their new awareness of how many Republicans across the country had been running unopposed and of the need to recruit candidates to challenge incumbents. Marchers spoke of sending postcards and making phone calls to elected representatives, of lobbying for increased funding to women's health organizations. Women were in it for the long haul. "Immediate outrage and sustained outrage are two different things," a protester named Sarah Jaffe told *Politico*. "I'm gearing up to be mad as hell for a long time."

One of the first official acts of the Trump presidency in January 2017 was to ban people from several predominantly Muslim nations from entering the country, and it was women who rose up in fury in response. Nabeela Syed from Illinois was a senior in high school at the time. As a practicing Muslim, she felt Trump's ban like a gut punch. "This is really how people feel about us," she recalled. "This is how people feel about Muslims. This is how people feel about women." She was angry, but she would not allow Trump's bigoted agenda to win. "That was when I was like, 'We could either let people talk about us this way, or we could be part of it, and we could create space in politics.'" After college, she started to get involved in local political races and eventually decided to run herself. "When people ask, I always tie it back to 2016, that moment when I was a senior in high school. I felt like I belonged in my high school. I wore a hijab. I was prom queen. I felt like I was on top of the world, and still, I could feel so small because the man who was elected president could spew that rhetoric."

What those first days of Trump's administration showed was that every attempt to cut women down was taken up as an opportunity for replenishing their fury. When Massachusetts Senator Elizabeth Warren stood on the Senate floor to oppose one of Trump's cabinet appointees, Republican Senate Majority Leader Mitch McConnell ordered her to stop, forcing her to leave the Senate floor. McConnell surely made this move as his own symbolic message to his base: that he was willing and able to shut down a mouthy woman and aggressive challenger to Republican policies. "She was warned," McConnell said of Warren's attempt to speak out. "She was given an explanation. Nevertheless, she persisted." The phrase blew up and became a kind of shorthand for tough women spanning the centuries, with memes attaching it to women as diverse as Harriet Tubman and the international activist for girls' education, Malala Yousafzai. One woman in Minneapolis persuaded more than a hundred of her friends and strangers to get "She persisted" tattoos. As Warren herself said on cable television: "They can shut me up, but they can't change the truth."

The perceived toppling of one threatening woman was provoking a million more—many of them a million times angrier than they'd ever been before—to raise their own voices. Here it was, an anger that was so intense it blazed its way even from the most official and respectable sources—women who were members of the House of Representatives, senators, mayors—anything to let people know this: Women. Were. Furious. After the election, everything that had been restrained and secret and muffled could no longer be contained beneath a veneer of "going high," or venting only to the like-minded. "Of all the feelings that have surfaced since January—sadness, depression, hopelessness, rare bits of joy," wrote the feminist journalist Samhita Mukhopadhyay at the end of 2017, "the one that has sustained, motivated and sometimes felt like it was destroying me has been anger." The British feminist Laurie Penny tweeted in July 2017, "Most of the interesting women you know are far, far angrier than you'd imagine."

Women signed up to run for office, in numbers higher than the country had ever seen. EMILYs List, an organization that raises money for pro-choice Democratic candidates, put the number at over forty thousand in the year and a half after the election. Many of them spoke openly of how it was their fury at Trump, about the fact that he'd won and what it had shown them about the biases and inequities that still existed, contrary to everything they'd been told, that had motivated them to throw their hats in the ring.

And then, in October 2017, not yet a year into the Trump presidency, the *New York Times* published a story about Harvey Weinstein, a movie producer accused of abusing and harassing women for decades. It was—while grotesque and a long time coming—not *so* different from other stories about other powerful men that had been published in recent years, stories that had attracted increasing interest, that had been taken, slowly, more seriously, but which had not changed the world or workplaces, or how they continued to function.

But American women were a tinderbox, and the Weinstein story was an extremely hot match. Suddenly the media, not to mention the women making it and consuming it, were newly aflame, many using the hashtag #metoo, in reference to a movement first started by the activist Tarana Burke in 2006 to address sexual violence particularly in Black and brown communities, but which got taken up in 2017 and applied more widely to the flood of revelations coming from every corner of the globe. Women were telling stories they'd never told aloud before, to reporters and to one another. And where moments like this had lasted, in the past, for a few days or weeks, what was most startling was that this movement just kept going . . . for weeks, then months. Some famous men, rich men, powerful men, lost their jobs after being accused of harassment and abuse.

The reemergence of women's rage as a mass impulse was here, after decades of feminist deep freeze. It was an eruption of so much that had been held back, hidden from view, for decades, for centuries. Something bad happened to you, you shoved it down, you maybe told someone but probably didn't get much satisfaction—emotional or practical—from the confession. Maybe you even got criticized. No one really cared, and certainly no one was going to do anything about it. But in the four months that followed the reporting on one movie mogul's sexual predation, the anger window was open. Ijeoma Oluo wrote in *Elle* in January 2018: "To the men scratching their heads in concern and confusion: The rage you see right now, the rage bringing down previously invulnerable men today, barely scratches the surface. You think we might be angry? You have no idea how angry we are."

"Grab the broom of anger and drive off the beast of fear," wrote the author Zora Neale Hurston in 1942, and I thought hard about that phrase through the fall of 2017. The anger that had propelled women into the streets in January and to the phones and protests and onto ballots through the spring was still burning, picking further fights. Anger was the broom that swept America's newly infuriated women into a new year, 2018, the year in which electoral opportunity provided a new channel for their furious drive.

A Repressed Majority

As America approached its two hundred and fiftieth year since revolution was declared, still just one hundred and fifty years since the abolition of slavery, a century since some women won the right to vote, and sixty years since African Americans secured civil rights and voting rights—all events that occurred in the wake of uprisings of Americans furious at the injustices they faced—women in America gathered in anger again. It was messy; it was divided—by race and age and political leanings. It was not civil; it was often profane. It was a mass fury: occasionally so frenzied that it made people nervous. Were it any other way, nothing would ever change.

This is the revolutionary mission, what the idealized vision of what this country might be was born of: the righteous fury of the unrepresented. We are taught that the furious expression of patriotism is a kind of birthright of the American people. Founders of the United States used passionate, striking phrases like *give me liberty or give me death*, *live free or die*, and *don't tread on me* as a way of rallying the people to their cause: freedom from the tyranny of the king of England. The governing documents they wrote and codified into law—the Declaration of Independence, the Constitution, and the Bill of Rights—grounded and lent legal weight to the notions of freedom, equality, and human dignity. But when people who were not wealthy, white, Christian, land-owning men tried to use those universal concepts to claim their rights, they were viewed not as admirable, reasonable, as the crucial driving ingredient to political change; they were instead condemned as threats. What our founders established was not a true representative democracy, but rather one in which a minority ruled, based on a myth of wide and just representation, and in which that minority benefited from the labor of and reduced competition from a subjugated majority. In order to maintain minority rule, the majority's resistance must be repressed, its anger discouraged.

And while women are expected to muffle their rage, there is no such expectation of men who are accused of doing the very things that made women so angry. During the height of #metoo, when harassers, abusers, and assaulters were called out, shamed, and punished, the reaction, all too often, was to center their feelings and needs. It's a disproportionate dynamic that the philosophy professor Kate Manne has called "himpathy," comparing the collective concern we muster about the men who drove women out of careers by harassing them till they fled to our comparative inability to imagine, let alone prioritize, the humanity of anyone who is not a Christian white male. The ability to flip the dynamics of aggression and abuse—to view the less powerful as a menace to the aggressors—has been key to how white patriarchal structures have persisted.

Women's anger, publicly and loudly expressed, is considered unnatural, chaotic, upsetting to how power is supposed to work. These structural assumptions are why calls for civility almost always help oppressors, because incivility against the oppressed is not only so normalized, it is also so comforting that it can barely be detected as oppression. Which is what made #metoo so fraught and revolutionary. It was a period during which some of the most powerful men faced consequences.

What happened in the second decade of the twenty-first century is that women began to rage publicly in ways that made them audible to one another; we began to hear one another and understand that we were not as alone or isolated in our rage as we had been led to believe. Whether it was about police violence, or the election of terrible politicians, or about gun violence, or about low wages, or about abortion, women began yelling, and the effect was—is—volcanic.

We must train ourselves to be able to see and hear anger from women and understand it not only as rational, but as politically meaningful. It is, in fact, an anger on behalf of the nation's suppressed majority and therefore especially frightening and explosive because of the threat it poses to the ruling minority. We are primed to hear the anger of men as stirring, downright American, as our national lullaby, and primed to hear the sound of women demanding freedom as the screech of nails on our national chalkboard. That's because women's full equality would in fact end white male dominance. And the resistance to that disruption of dominance is itself so potent that we are now in the throes of resistance to it: Those who want to stay in charge treat women's uprising as hysteria, a mob, a witch hunt, a passing phase, a childish tantrum, something irrational, something we'd be better off without if everyone can just calm down.

There will be claims that the anger is not authentic but performed.

There will be tremendous pressure to not take it seriously, to not listen too carefully to what the loud, shrill voices are saying, insistence that women giving voice to their rage are sure to lose, or are simply working to provoke further discrimination and disregard. Women's anger will be—as it long has been—cast as ugly, unappealing, dangerous, something to be shut down or booed. Nothing, we long have been assured, is more unattractive in a woman than anger, and those messages will be especially damaging—as they have always been—to nonwhite women. But these are all strategies that have long been used to get people, including women themselves, to look away from, disregard, and suppress one of the great drivers of social upheaval and political change in this country: their own fury.

Backlash

Everyone, including me, was waiting for the backlash from practically the first moment that #metoo kicked off. With every new article published that was critical of #metoo came the tremor of a question: Was this it? The backlash? Enough of us knew enough about our history to know that it was on its way. Any minute, coming to swallow us up and feed us to Phyllis Schlafly's ghost for dinner before we knew what hit us. Laurie Penny wrote, "We know what happens when women get out of control, don't we?"

Yes. That's when we change the world.

To some extent, women who wanted liberty and equality knew they had to create some chaos. And yes, it was moving with such velocity and intensity that it was terrifying in its unpredictability. But it had to be radical and wrathful and energetic to get people to pay attention and to actually alter the power dynamics. Rules had to be changed, as they had been in the Second Wave of feminism during the 1970s, when marriages entered into on unequal terms were no longer acceptable and the fact that some of them ended was a sudden shock to the system and some men felt they had been unfairly victimized by swiftly changing expectations. Now unwanted groping and lewd remarks and harassment were no longer going to be acceptable and some men were going to lose their jobs and some of them would no doubt feel that they had been unfairly victimized.

But this was what it meant to say that we wanted the world to be different: not in some hazy future after all the old not-different men had retired from their perches and died peacefully in their sleep. We wanted it to be different now, and that meant dethroning some of them early. Things had to get out of control. "The law cannot do it for us," Shirley Chisholm had said years earlier. "We must do it for ourselves. Women in this country must become revolutionaries."

In the view of Catharine MacKinnon, a crusading legal scholar who fought sexual harassment, the surging #metoo movement itself was an "uprising of the formerly disregarded." It demonstrated an unwillingness to look away any longer. And the anger it had drawn forth was shifting what the law had not been able to: the culture. Disgust with "harassing behavior . . . could change workplaces and schools. It could restrain repeat predators as well as the occasional and casual exploiters that the law so far has not."

That was what many women wanted: a remaking of the structure, of the systems and the institutions. And it wasn't such an outlandish request. Because all around us, in special elections and in primaries, women were running for office. And winning. Perhaps #metoo wasn't going to be about retribution; rather it might be about *replacement*.

On election night in the fall of 2017, Virginia seated a record number of women in its general assembly, including its first Asian American woman, its first two Latina women, and its first transgender woman, Danica Roem, who had run against the Virginia delegate who had written the state's transphobic bill barring trans people from using bathrooms that best suited their gender identities. In New Jersey, Ashley Bennett had run against a Republican city county freeholder because he'd openly mocked women who'd attended the women's march—via a meme asking whether the protest would end in time for them to cook him dinner—and beaten him.

Watching the election returns, I got a text from an old friend, a woman who'd worked on the 2016 Clinton campaign and who'd been there next to me, shell-shocked, on that night that Clinton had lost. She told me she'd been crying while watching the Virginia results come in.

"Maybe *we're* the backlash," she wrote.

• *13* •

The Exhilaration of Activism

I'm turning my anger into action.

I'm trying to convert my anger into inspiration.

I've taken my anger and channeled it into activism.

My anger has hardened into determination.

Do a Google image search on any powerful women in politics or public life, especially those who threaten white male power—by pressing for reforms in the military, the criminal justice system, the banking industry, or by running for office to beat powerful men—and you'll turn up scores of photos of them with their mouths open, unrestrained: mid-yell, the very act of making a loud noise a sign of their ugly and unnatural personalities. The best way to discredit these women, to make them look unattractive, is to capture an image of them screaming; the act of a woman opening her mouth with volume and assured force, often in complaint, is coded in our minds as ugly.

Perhaps the negativity around the yelling woman goes back to the disproportionate labor they perform as caretakers of the young, and women's raised voices an unhappy reminder of getting in trouble, tones that make men feel like children again, under the punishing thumbs of their mothers, grandmothers, older sisters, nannies, and teachers who nurtured and educated them. "We're raised by women," said Gloria Steinem, "so we experience female power when we're younger. And men, especially, when they see a powerful woman as an adult, feel regressed to childhood and strike out at her."

But the way in which adult female scolding may return some men to a youthful, domestic sphere of the home—the only one in which women have been granted a kind of unchallenged power—speaks to what women's full-throated challenge does: It turns things upside down, reminds us of a time and place where women had authority. But when it's happening in politics, or in workplaces, or in activism, or elsewhere in the public sphere, it's considered not normal, an aberration, inappropriate. In this way, women's angry voices, raised in challenge to power structures, vibrate with the threat of insurgency, of revolution.

What these women seem to represent is a kind of disorder. And here there is a deep historical echo: In early twentieth-century propaganda film strips about suffragists, women demanding the basic right to vote are shown leaving their babies at home with their incapable husbands. Nature has been turned upside down; the women's fury at their exclusion from civic participation has provoked disorder in the home. Women's anger in any political context remains coded as chaotic, while men's is understood as rational and often admirable.

This is probably why, as I was reporting for this book, nearly every woman I spoke to described her anger as a thing of the past. "I *was* angry," an interviewee would say, "but I'm not angry anymore; I've taken my anger and turned it into action." Anger had to have been felt in the past tense in order to be something that many women I spoke to could describe to me with authority or confidence, let alone enthusiasm. About ten minutes into every interview I did in which a woman had assured me that she'd cast off her anger, I'd find her cursing and raising her voice, yelling about how livid she was: at her father, or her friends, or more broadly, at the nation and its injustices. These women were angry; *of course* they were angry. But they were conditioned to deny it from the start. This was something I heard again and again: the desire to take anger and transform it into something else, something that was *not* anger.

But anger should not *need* to be transformed in order to count as worthy; anger on its own can have progressive value. As Amanda Litman, a Clinton campaign staffer who after the election launched an organization called Run for Something, which recruits and supports young Americans running for office, has written, "Instead of resisting [anger] or avoiding it, let your fury push you to action. Embrace your anger and put it to work."

Around the world, angry women have come up with innovative forms of protest and expression. Some of the ideas are very old, some are brand-new; some will transform the world, others will fail. But the fury is moving women and their thinking on inequality forward. And sometimes the anger is working its magic simply by existing, persisting, unrelenting and unapologetic. In political organizing, the impact of women's anger after 2016 was profound.

Erin Vilardi, the head of VoteRunLead, which trains and supports women running for state and local office, had a theory about what happened after election night 2016: "It turns out those were angry tears everybody cried on November 8, and nobody knew they were angry tears until later," she said. She also noted that until recently, women have had no road map for what to do with their resentments and furies. "Women are not allowed to scream from podiums, not allowed to slam doors in workplaces," she said, acknowledging that this expressive limit is part of what's earned women the reputation as nicer bosses. But that wasn't true, she went on. "Because if you look at all those studies about how women are better bosses, they're better at everything *except* in areas of decisiveness, and that's because we don't get to *have* that split-second, I'm-the-goddamn-boss-that's-why gut reaction. We have zero role modeling in channeling our anger into decisiveness or 'That's just the way he is' stuff people said about Harvey Weinstein. We don't get *any* of those passes."

But since Hillary Clinton's loss to Donald Trump in 2016, angry women began to flex their organizing muscles. New groups sprang up, including Run for Something and Sister District, which matches energetic volunteers in progressive areas that vote Democratic with "sister" races in right-wing Republican districts that need more fundraising and volunteer help. There was the Movement Voter Project to funnel donations to local progressive organizing groups; Indivisible, which organizes activists to get involved in campaigns; and Spread the Vote, which organizes volunteers to help prospective voters get the materials they need to obtain legal identification in states with restrictive voter ID laws.

These groups joined organizations that had long been on the

ground, including Emerge America and Higher Heights, with programs to recruit and train female candidates, young candidates, progressive candidates, and candidates of color to run for office in places and at levels the party had ignored for decades. The media's slow but steady acknowledgment of Black women's foundational, leading roles in progressive and feminist politics spurred boosts in attention to organizations like Higher Heights, cofounded by Kimberly Peeler-Allen, and Jessica Byrd's Three Point Strategies, which aim to center issues of racial justice and transform them into electoral victories for Black women running for mayor, for House seats, for the Senate, and to fill governors' mansions.

In campaigns over the last decade, newly angry moms brought skills they'd learned in their Parent-Teacher Associations to canvassing to get voters engaged and to the polls and organizing campaigns, registering thousands of new voters. And they even changed how campaigns operated. Liuba Grechen Shirley, who entered politics after the 2016 election, successfully petitioned the Federal Election Commission to be able to use campaign funds to pay for childcare, a potentially game-changing structural shift for women candidates who happen to be mothers. "I was enraged," she said of her entrance into politics and her realization, as she was mounting a campaign while trying to juggle and pay for care of two young children, about "why there are so many millionaires in office."

Angry Candidates Make the Best Candidates

"Let's make a full-blown trend out of replacing predatory men with women who were long overdue to hold their jobs in the first place," one writer crowed in *Vogue*. "It's really the least the patriarchy can do."

Of course, in most fields, altering power ratios is neither swift nor easy. Even when problematic men are pushed from lofty perches, those waiting to take their places, the ones who've accumulated seniority, expertise, and connections, still tend to be mostly men. Women who've been driven out or self-exiled from their chosen professions often cannot simply reenter them—not as leaders or managers or even mid-level employees.

This is one of the relative virtues of politics: It can be swiftly responsive to change. People can run for local or state or even federal office, even if they've never been so much as student council secretary. If they're preschool teachers or law professors or sanitation workers, there will be substantial obstacles—yes, weaker networks, fundraising disadvantages, and identity bias—to push past. Yes. But they can run. And if they win, whether the office is small or large, they might be able to shake things up. Between 1931, when Hattie Wyatt Caraway of Arkansas was appointed to fill her husband's seat as senator, and 1992, only six women had ever served in the United States Senate for more than about a year. In 1992, four women were elected to the Senate, tripling the number of women in that chamber; today more than one in four US Senators is a woman. In 2018, all previous records were broken. That year 476 women ran for seats in the House of Representatives, a number higher than any other time in American history. According to the Black Women in American Politics database, forty-seven Black women ran for federal seats in total, at least twenty-four of whom did not already hold seats in Congress running for the House of Representatives, then home to only twenty Black women. Kelly Dittmar at Rutgers University's Center for American Women and Politics has cautioned that that historic number still only represented 22 percent of the total number of House candidates. More women running does not always translate to more women winning. Everything is still changing. There is no predicting.

And yet.

The rise felt meaningful, and 2018 saw wave after wave of long-shot primary wins by underestimated women, many of them non-white, sometimes against entire fields of men. Everywhere you turned, there were women running for office for the first time—Democrats against Republicans but also angry liberal women challenging the men, and some of the other women, in their own parties. One of the most famous was Alexandria Ocasio-Cortez, then a twenty-eight-year-old former organizer for Bernie Sanders running on a Democratic Socialist platform who staged a shocking upset of ten-term incumbent New York City congressman Joe Crowley.

"Women have been the leaders of the resistance" to Donald Trump, said Lauren Underwood, a Black woman first elected to the House of Representatives in 2018, in a podcast interview when she was first running for that office. "Part of the reason that we're seeing women running is we know that our voices are needed to see the change we're looking for," she said, "because we can't count on someone else to be the advocate." Underwood is now serving in her fourth term in Congress.

Representative Lucy McBath became an anti-gun-violence organizer in the wake of her son's 2012 murder and flipped her Georgia House district in 2018 from Republican to Democrat. At the

Democratic convention in 2024, she spoke to me of the sincerity of purpose, and yes, emotion, that propelled women in 2018 to run and win, because constituents could relate to them. "I think it's because a lot of us didn't have any intentions of ever being in office. We bring our lived experiences, our different realities."

In the wake of #metoo, and the view it offered of the corroded and corrupted layer of male power, women had already stepped into political space left by men. It felt like an avenue toward something like the unimaginable: reparations for all the power that had been denied to women for so many centuries. "What if women hadn't been taken out of the pool like this?" asked Erin Vilardi.

Juliana Bennett was motivated to run for the common council in Madison, Wisconsin, during her junior year of college in 2021, enraged by the police killing the year before of George Floyd, a Black man walking out of a convenience store in Minneapolis. "I was very angry, very angry at the system, very angry at all the people that were still upholding the system. I remember I went from just being a protester to actually starting organized protests." She won the seat. While fury has long motivated her, she is ambivalent about it: "I have a weird relationship with anger, or the term angry specifically, because, especially as a young Black woman, you can easily fall into that angry Black woman category and then just completely get dismissed." And yet, "if someone calls me angry, I kind of get even more pissed."

Despite the efforts to suppress or disguise anger, Amanda Litman said she believed that angry candidates make the *best* candidates, because their passion propels them out the door every day to do the work of knocking on doors and making calls, producing the most crucial result: getting out the vote. In the 2018 governor's race in Virginia, the first-time women candidates had done such a stellar, driven job of canvassing and pavement-pounding that they had produced a higher turnout and helped Democrat Ralph Northam defeat Republican Ed Gillespie for governor. "Getting those candidates out there knocking [on] doors, speaking from a place of fury and commitment to change, gets more voters up, drives up turnout," said Litman.

Anger certainly fueled Nabeela Syed to run and to get others to run for office too. After she was elected to the Illinois General Assembly, she recalled being outraged by the demeaning behavior of a Republican colleague. At first she felt almost paralyzed by her anger—until she realized she could do something with it. "That anger kick-started me into action." She remembered thinking, "He doesn't deserve to be here." She started making plans to recruit someone better to run against him. "We don't need to settle for this," she said. "We can use that to change things."

Run As You Are

"When we started," said Patricia Russo, the head of the Women's Campaign School at Yale, which had begun training women candidates in 1994, in the wake of the 1992 Year of the Woman, "the median age for women attending our school was mid-forties. Now the median age is around thirty." That shift reflected new attitudes about when women were "allowed" to enter politics. They didn't have to wait until their kids were grown anymore, and there was a better chance that they'd be taken seriously in their thirties or even twenties—being young and single was no longer a deal-killer, nor was being the mother of little children. Also different now, Russo said, is that the majority of those who enroll in the school are women of color.

Other groups had also gotten into the candidate-training-and-support business over the past two decades and registered explosive growth in the wake of 2016. For Higher Heights—founded in 2011 to harness the power of Black women as voters, organizers, and candidates—a slow rise in engagement in the months after Trump's win became an enormous spike with the fall 2017 elections in Virginia, New Jersey, and Alabama, when the role of Black women *voters* as responsible for Democratic wins had been noted by the political media. "Black women were really acknowledged as political drivers of change, as first-time candidates and as the voters who made the difference," said cofounder Kimberly Peeler-Allen.

VoteRunLead's Erin Vilardi said that in a typical year, two-thirds of the organization's resources were devoted to persuading women to run, with a goal of tapping two thousand nationwide. In 2017 alone, 3,200 women were trained by VoteRunLead, and over ten thousand had contacted the group on their own. EMILYs List, meanwhile, had nearly tripled the size of its state and local team and doubled its digital staff to handle the forty thousand inquiries they'd received about jumping into the electoral fray post-Trump.

"I think there's a disgust," Vilardi said, "when women find themselves running against a guy who hasn't changed the photo on his website since the 1990s—these men have been in office for so long." Then there was another kind of disgust, increasingly articulated by at least some of the rookie politicians she'd met: "There's disgust very much about the abuse that men in power have systematically been engaging in unchecked, and disgust with the people who continue to keep those men in power."

The throng of disgusted women, most of them brand-new to politics, did require the investment of time and resources. And many of the mechanisms in place to train women candidates were quickly at capacity, thanks to the rush of women who knew mostly that they were furious but did not know much beyond that. "If you wake up in the morning caring about something," Emily Cain of EMILYs List told a group of potential candidates, notepads out, in 2017, "you are qualified to run for office." The message echoed one delivered by Higher Heights cofounder Peeler-Allen to the Black women she advises, many of whom lack confidence: "Each one of you is beyond prepared to run for public office. You need to channel your inner mediocre white boy and use that to run."

The whole training curriculum of VoteRunLead was overhauled in 2017 and could be summed up with its call to action: "Run As You Are." Vilardi mentioned Eve Hurwitz, a navy reservist and small-business owner running for state senator in Maryland. She'd long colored her hair a vivid shade of purple, but, said Vilardi, "Everybody told her that you can't run with purple hair, so she lost it, but other people said, 'How are you not going to run with purple hair? That's who you are!' So she dyed it back." Similarly, Peeler-Allen recalled reassuring a recent candidate who was fretting about whether she had to code-switch—alter her speaking style and mannerisms—to speak before different audiences. "Be genuine in what you're saying," Peeler-Allen said she advised. "As long as people feel you have their best interests at heart, it won't matter whether you twang or drawl or drop a consonant here or there."

Which is not to say that the political waters would suddenly part, allowing women to walk serenely into office. But for all the obstacles first-time female candidates face, Vilardi noticed a refreshingly new mindset post 2016. "The 'Am I qualified?' stuff we used to hear, when women would talk themselves out of running for office—what is the time management going to be, wondering how they'll talk to their husband or partner or boss about this, worrying that they can't make this work with their job, or that legislatures pay low wages—now all of that is being negotiated in a positive way." Instead of talking themselves out of it, they were talking themselves into it. "It's like lightbulbs are going off everywhere," Vilardi said.

Part of it was a feeling of urgency in response to what had recently been exposed, after years of the myth that sexism was in decline. And the shift in attitudes hit suddenly. When Tresa Undem conducted a poll in December 2016 asking if the Trump campaign and election had made voters "think more about sexism in our society," 40 percent of respondents said yes. Less than a year later, in November 2017, when she asked whether the news about sexual harassment and assault made people think more about societal sexism, 73 percent said that it did. In December 2016, 52 percent of those surveyed by Undem said that the country would be better off with more women in office; in November 2017, 69 percent gave that answer. And in 2016, 65 percent of people Undem polled felt that men held more positions of power in society than women; in 2017, that number rose to 87 percent. "As pollsters, we don't see shifts in attitudes this big," Undem said, also noting that women were using the word "misogyny," a word she'd rarely, if ever, heard in previous years.

The sight of so many women rushing to occupy elected office was almost sure to draw out opposition. All reassurances to the contrary, this is a zero-sum game: If women gain greater political power, white men lose some of theirs. Andrea Steele of Emerge America, which trains Democratic women candidates in twenty-four states, worked on Carol Moseley Braun's campaign in 1992 and remembered the drop-off in women candidates that happened *after* 1992. "We thought everything was going to change," she said, recalling the deep disappointment when it didn't. "The difference between then and now is we have infrastructure . . . there are state organizations helping to fund candidates. And a big part of what we've seen over the years is that when women get into politics, they start bringing other women in."

While the vision of women storming the ramparts of government was radical from one vantage point, it was as American as the idea of representative democracy laid out by our forefathers. "Representative citizens coming from all parts of the nation, cobblers and farmers—that was what was intended by the founders," said Marie Newman, a former small-business owner and anti-bullying advocate who challenged longtime opponent of abortion rights Illinois incumbent Democrat Dan Lipinski in a 2018 primary and came close to beating him. "You come to the House for a while and bring your ideas and then you probably go back to your life."

What Newman and her fellow female candidates were challenging were often the structural realities of patriarchal power in its purest form: Her opponent had been in office himself for thirteen years, and his father had held the same seat for twenty years before that. Of course he had been elected, but his family name and generations in power had helped make his campaign victories almost inevitable. "It's a family that has reigned supreme, like a monarchy, for over thirty years," Newman said during her race, her frustration with the bonkers unfairness of it unhidden. "He's an old white man who doesn't understand what his district wants, and it doesn't matter what party you're in. We are more than half the population, but only twenty percent of Congress."

And while Marie Newman did not win that primary, the closeness of the race, against such an entrenched example of inherited white male power, offered some hope that it could be done. And it was. In 2020 Newman beat Lipinski in the Democratic primary and went on to win the House seat in the general election.

That same election cycle, Kamala Harris ran for president, inspired by one of her role models: "We stand on the shoulders of Shirley Chisholm and Shirley Chisholm stood proud," she said. Harris did not win the nomination for the presidency, but later, as Joe Biden's running mate, she did break one of the highest and hardest glass ceilings, becoming the first woman, the first African American, and the first Asian American to be elected vice president of the United States.

• 14 •

In the Soup

Forced Labor

But as was true over centuries of American history, backlash to the kind of progress that disrupts power can be brutal. Just as American women were beginning to feel that the ground was truly starting to shift, that they might even achieve a new measure of equality with these election victories, a Supreme Court ruling came down to once again push them back.

On June 24, 2022, the US Supreme Court, in *Dobbs v. Jackson Women's Health Organization*, overturned *Roe v. Wade*, the 1973 ruling that protected a woman's right to abortion. The six-to-three ruling against women's freedoms and equality would not have been possible but for three new right-wing justices who had been appointed by President Trump, a man whose election had itself been fueled by backlash anger at the growing power of women and Black people, and which had in turn spurred an activist wave.

Dobbs did not come as a surprise to those who had been paying attention, those with their hair on fire who had been told for decades that their fear was theatrical, unhinged, overdramatic.

Those who'd been paying attention knew that the efforts to reinstall women back at home, strip them of their abilities to control their bodies, their families, their economic and professional prospects, had been building as they took up more space in public, professional, and political spheres.

The dissent in opposition to the ruling, coauthored by the Supreme Court's three liberal judges, was explicit. "Whatever the exact scope of the coming laws, one result of today's decision is certain: the curtailment of women's rights, and of their status as free and equal citizens." They wrote that, in the wake of this decision, "from the very moment of fertilization, a woman has no rights to speak of. A state can force her to bring a pregnancy to term, even at the steepest personal and familial costs."

The *Dobbs* ruling not only inflicted serious harm but ensured that the job of protecting abortion rights and access must be undertaken legislatively—Congress has to pass laws to ensure that women have access to abortion care. It's different work than it was in 1972 before *Roe v. Wade*: Medication abortion, data-tracking technology, and political divisiveness have all altered the terrain. And it took no time for the *Dobbs* ruling to unleash a wave of restrictions on access to abortion in the states. Within two years of the ruling, one in three American women of reproductive age lived in a state with severe limits on abortion and reproductive health care.

But like the cycles of progress and regress that had come before, *Dobbs* also sparked an electoral revolution in the politics of abortion. In the wake of the ruling, Democrats pulled off unlikely victories—in conservative "red" states and liberal "blue" states and in oddly timed off-year contests—because of abortion. They won state supreme court seats, legislative majorities, governor's races, and a string of referendum votes on the issue. On Election Day 2023, voters approved a state constitutional protection of abortion in Ohio, rejected Virginia's Republican governor Glenn Youngkin's promise of a fifteen-week abortion ban, reelected pro-choice Democratic governor Andy Beshear in Kentucky, and chose a justice who vowed to protect abortion rights for Pennsylvania's supreme court.

Michigan perhaps exemplified this ideal for Democrats. Governor Gretchen Whitmer, who initiated legal action to protect abortion in the state in advance of *Dobbs*, ran in 2022 alongside a ballot initiative and on a bold promise to protect abortion access. After winning control of the state legislature and governorship, Michigan Democrats protected the right to abortion in the state constitution, repealed a ban from 1931, and passed a Reproductive Health Act that removes some remaining barriers to abortion care. It's a virtuous cycle: Politicians made pledges, voters believed them enough to empower them, and the politicians followed through. "These are hard-fought victories on the ballot," says Whitmer, "but also hard-fought work on a legislative level. It's one thing to be on the right side of a fight and another to take the action after you've won the fight."

Voters and these elected leaders cobbled together a path forward, spurred by anger at the *Dobbs* ruling and a refusal to let despair win. This is a crucial reminder in times of punitive political regress, under regimes that want to drain the populace of hope: Despair is poison. It deadens people when the most important thing they can do is proceed with more drive and force and openness than they have before. Which is why the work ahead is insisting on hope, behaving as if there is *reason* to hope for better, even if you feel, based on the abundant available evidence, that there is not.

People who have been battling through injustice and inequity for a long time have built networks and mechanisms. They run clinics and funds and have experience helping people get the care they need when that care has been denied and obstructed by the state. They have developed the medicines, pioneered the delivery systems, and familiarized themselves with the laws. One of the people doing this work, Debasri Ghosh, the managing director of the National Network of Abortion Funds, told me in the wake of the *Dobbs* decision, "Beyond abortion, I have been thinking a lot about how so many of us in this movement, particularly Black and brown and Indigenous folks, have ancestries and histories of resistance. We have this lineage of fighting back against hard-won rights being regressed, fighting back against going backwards. It is important for us to be able to tell those stories much more broadly. And we have to look to that ancestral wisdom to be able to find a path forward." This is the muscle memory of those who have never had the comfort that their rights would remain intact.

This country's history has been built on bad days like June 24, 2022. Its people—those willing to give their lives and every scrap of hope they could muster—have reformed it by the force of their anger. So while we weep and mourn and rage about this injustice, we also go forward with the will of those who came before, and those who have never stopped putting one foot in front of another, to some finer tomorrow, distant but always possible.

My Sisters Are Here

Change won't come simply from the women who have over the past decade decided to run for office or started new organizations; it will also come from the women who are engaging in their campaigns, volunteering, paying attention, educating themselves, becoming activists. The self-styled "Resistance" that grew up in response to the first Donald Trump administration was made of, built on, the efforts of women. Yes, progressive politics had long relied on the labor of women, many of them women of color, the hardworking base of state and local political organizing. But what happened after Clinton's loss, and grew through the #metoo movement, and the fury over mass shootings, the rage about limits to abortion rights, was the activation of another population, long inactive: suburban white women.

Their activism led to the election of a new generation of lawmakers who better reflect the priorities of this moment, who better integrate what long were isolated as "women's issues" to a position of centrality in elections. The new messaging on abortion rights is an example. But activists and elected officials also realize that they can never just pat themselves on the back and assume that their victories will hold. "We can't make the mistake that our predecessors did," Governor Gretchen Whitmer told me, "that just because we've made an advancement that it's the new floor." Majorities change. Leaders move on. Whitmer says she's working with an eye toward what happens when "you get a different legislature and governor, that they don't try to bring that back to life again." And indeed, in the 2024 election that brought Trump back to office, Whitmer lost her state legislative trifecta; she will be term-limited out of office in 2026.

But perhaps this too is a generational shift, the awareness of the shortcomings of our governing institutions, which means making the most of the time in power and preparing for what follows, and never assuming that the fight is done. "We amended the constitution of Michigan; we are safe for now," said Whitmer, before what would be that devastating presidential loss of 2024, an election cycle in which Democrats lost power not just in Washington and Michigan, but around the country. "But if there's a national ban, we're back in the soup. We've got to make sure people understand that this fight is not over. It is happening state by state right now, but it's going to continue to be a national fight. People in solidly blue states who think, Abortion is safe in my town or in my state? It's not." This is one of the most important post-*Roe* lessons. The belief in a kind of Forever Progress was what led too many to believe that there was nothing to worry about. It has prevented a proper understanding of this country's history and its foundational power imbalances. As Congresswoman Barbara Lee told me, "If you are in this thing just for a minute? Goodbye. You just have to figure out how to keep at it."

It takes endurance to remain "in the soup," but angry women seem up for the task. "If I'm not knocking on doors, I'm making calls; if I'm not making calls, I'm writing postcards; if I'm not writing postcards, I'm replacing my lawn sign," I heard one woman say at a suburban restaurant outside Atlanta in 2017 during a special election race there. She and her peers were using a language of awakening and liberation that was reminiscent of past insurgencies.

"I am no longer in the closet," Ann White, a sixty-four-year-old former speech pathologist told me back in 2018. "I am out, I am out blue.

Everybody knows now that I'm a Democrat, that I'm liberal. And they're kind of tired of it, but that's okay. I'm not done. I'm just getting started." White, like so many previously unworried white women, had simply believed that Hillary Clinton would beat Donald Trump in 2016. When she hadn't, White said, she had felt herself transforming. "The profanity filter on my mouth totally went away," she said, recalling cursing like a sailor on the phone with a friend, shocking her teenage children, who'd "never heard me say the F-word before." She attended the Women's March in Atlanta, and said that "it was the very first time since the election that I felt empowered." She also realized, for the first time, that "there's a whole lot of people like me who are not going to take this lying down!"

This is one of anger's most important roles: It is a mode of connection, a way for women to find one another and realize that their struggles and their frustrations are shared, that they are not alone, not crazy. If they are quiet, they will remain isolated. But if they howl in rage, someone else who shares their fury might hear them, might start howling along. This is, of course, partly why those who oppress women work to stifle their anger.

Woman after woman spoke to me of how the loud eruption of their rage had brought them into a community they'd never known existed. Women spoke with the youthful fervor of having found new friends and new love—of politics and one another. Several described how they'd not been sleeping, staying up all night scrolling through Facebook and message boards, reading political posts and messaging one another. Fifty-one-year-old Tamara Brooking told me, "I'm done. I'm done pretending that your hateful rhetoric is okay. I'm done pretending that people like us must be quiet to make you feel comfortable." There's that willingness to make others uncomfortable; it turns everything upside down, disturbs the equilibrium of households and partnerships that had been built around making nice and keeping quiet. And in this, too, there were other kinds of reminders of the Second Wave, the kinds of intimate upheavals it had provoked.

Dawn Penich-Thacker was driven in the wake of Trump's election in 2016 to become more civically involved, led a petition to reverse a program in Arizona that would have cut school funding, and assisted in the teachers' strike there in 2018. Her relationships with her fellow activists, she said, "are the deepest friendships I've ever had. These women in this movement are my battle buddies. I can't imagine leaving this behind, even if it ravaged my life."

A Moment of Joy

"That is a moment of joy," Vivian Gornick wrote in 1990, looking back at the 1970s, "when a sufficiently large number of people . . . are gathered together in the same place at the same time, speaking the same language, making the same analysis, meeting again and again in restaurants, lecture halls and apartments. . . . It is the joy of revolutionary politics, and it was ours. To be a feminist in New York City in the early '70s—bliss was it in that dawn to be alive. Not an I-love-you in the world could touch it. There was no other place to be, except with each other. We lived then, all of us, inside the loose embrace of feminism. It was as though we'd been released from a collective lifetime of silence."

"I believe this is the beginning of a new wave of feminism," activist Jennifer Mosbacher told me in 2018. "And I hope by the time my nine-year-old daughter is in college, she'll be reading books about this movement and how it changed the tide in this country."

By 2018, the rising generation of activists seemed to be absorbing these messages faster than their foremothers and forefathers ever had. The March for Our Lives, held in March 2018 and organized by the high school students of Parkland, Florida, in the wake of the mass shooting at their school, was a model of interconnected anger. Officially a protest against gun violence and the NRA's grip on American politics, its speakers seemed to see it as all part of one piece: "We need to arm our teachers with . . . the money they need to support their families and to support themselves,'" said one speaker, while eleven-year-old Naomi Wadler named the too-often forgotten names of African American girls "whose stories don't make the front page of every newspaper." The furious young activist X González dared to make everyone terribly uncomfortable by holding them in silence, without explanation or apology, until the six and a half minutes it had taken for a student to kill seventeen classmates had ticked out.

The protest felt effortlessly integrated in its concerns. Signs about gun violence acknowledged how deeply white patriarchy was embedded in the crisis of mass shootings, and read things like "White Men Are Terrifying (Statistically)" and "Your Guns Have More Rights Than My Vagina" and "We Live in a Country Where Guns Matter More Than Black Women's Lives." Common rapped, "I stand for peace, love, and women's rights." One young woman, nervous about speaking in front of millions, simply leaned over in the middle of her speech and vomited, while speakers wept, and their noses ran; it was astounding, moving to see the guts of girls' passions on display, without apology or shame—its own testament to urgency and fury and the will to change.

The scene reminded me of the fierce impatience of Tokata Iron Eyes. "Everyone is sitting around waiting for somebody else to do something. And the thing about it is that it will never happen unless you start," she told the writer Tess Thomas. But her sense of urgency doesn't make action any less scary or daunting to undertake. "I get scared every time. I get scared every time before I speak, but I think that there's really a lot of power in being scared and doing something anyway." The commitment to speaking because your head and heart tell you so is a kind of model, its own reflection on the value of dissent, letting emotion and reason shape your message because your heart and your head are legitimate. "And if I have something that I need to say that's not being said then why not me? Why not my voice?"

Tokata Iron Eyes, Naomi Wadler, X González, all recalled the explosive drive behind a 1917 statement written by Lavinia Dock, a suffragist, called "The Young Are At The Gates," a phrase that would become the National Women's Party banner in the suffrage fight.

"What is the potent spirit of youth?" Dock asked. "Is it not the spirit of revolt, of rebellion against senseless and useless and deadening things? Most of all, against injustice, which is of all stupid things the stupidest? Such thoughts come to one in looking over the field of the Suffrage campaign and watching the pickets at the White House and at the Capitol, where sit the men who complacently enjoy the rights they deny to the women at their gates . . . A fatal error—a losing fight. The old stiff minds must give way. The old selfish minds must go. Obstructive reactionaries must move on. The young are at the gates!"

As I've interviewed young people for this book, I have encountered this spirit again and again. While anger is definitely a motivating factor in their activism, so is solidarity, finding community, and, crucially, as Gornick wrote in the 1990s, joy. Because these young people have an almost innate understanding that their struggles—whether against climate change, trans hate, gun violence, or for women's bodily autonomy and basic freedoms—will be lifelong. Fifteen-year-old Daniel Trujillo and thirteen-year-old Libby Gonzalez, two trans youths, brought that attitude to the first ever trans prom they organized on Capitol Hill in Washington, DC, in the spring of 2023. Daniel told me about their motivation, that he and Libby "were really frustrated and angry about all the legislation that we've been having to continuously deal with since we were born. So then we needed a political action."

Libby, who has been an activist since she was six, was frustrated, terrified, and furious about the hundreds of anti-trans laws that were being introduced around the country even before Donald Trump's reelection, laws that were targeting her for her very existence. "Prom was a way of reclaiming our stories," Libby said. Libby, Daniel, and their friends know they'll be in this for the long haul, so they wanted prom to be fun, too, not only to strengthen their bonds to one another and have a good time, but for the added benefit of needling their tormentors. Daniel said, "So all of these Republicans and all these conservatives are really trying to make it harder for us and really trying to push our buttons, ruin our days, take away our rights. So I thought the funniest thing would be to do a party outside of their office window and have all of us smiling and yelling and dancing while they are stuck in the little offices. What are they going to do? So I was like, it can be joyous for the community and also really funny. It was charged in all the right ways," he said, "emotionally."

Since 2018, it has been both the literally and the more metaphorically young—those whose willingness to give voice to rage was budding—who were at the gates, challenging the men who enjoy the rights they deny others.

As Ann White, the suburban Georgia sixty-four-year-old woman who'd been newly woken from her slumber of political indifference, told me, she was feeling the responsibility of taking a stand, not on her own behalf, but "for people of color, for those who cannot afford health insurance, who are lesbian, gay, and transgender, for immigrants. I'm a white older woman. There's a lot of old white people that are on [the Republican] side right now. Well, I'm an old white person and I can be vocal too."

"It's so powerful and kind of reminds me that the other side of the anger is the hope," Jessica Morales, who had worked on Hillary Clinton's 2016 campaign, wrote to me. "We wouldn't be angry if we didn't still believe that it could be better."

And if it gets better in part because of women's ability and willingness and need to feel their anger and to let it out into the world, then what we would be living through right now would not be a trend or a fad or a witch hunt, but an insurrection—a righteous revolution, led by angry women.

Long Live the Resistance

In 2024, President Joe Biden was determined to run for reelection despite his old age, his promise to be a "bridge president" to the next generation, and terrible poll numbers that reflected his unpopularity. But when he badly flubbed a debate against Donald Trump in June, he relented to mounting pressure to exit the race and endorsed his vice president, Kamala Harris, to run as the Democratic nominee. With only one hundred days until Election Day, Harris led a purposefully joyful campaign that was at its start framed around freedom, including a focus on reproductive freedom and abortion rights.

Harris's initial approach to the fight was rooted in the women-of-color-led reproductive-justice movement, linking abortion rights to other inequities, including the country's high maternal mortality rates, which reflect an unacceptably high number of women who die while giving birth, and lack of affordable housing, paid leave for working parents who have a baby, and childcare availability. In 2023, Harris told me she came to the abortion battle "as someone raised by parents who were active in the civil rights movement and a mother who fought for women's health issues." Abortion rights, she said, are based on "our collective ability to exercise self-determination," noting that people's "freedom to make certain decisions about their own life, and who they love, and their own bodies—those are the attributes of a democracy."

In rally after rally during the summer and fall of 2024, Harris would detail the dangers posed by a potential second Trump presidency to women, to workers, to children, to the economy, to freedom and democracy itself, and then wrap up saying simply, "We're not going back." Her massive crowds would cheer wildly in response and chant "We're not going back! We're not going back!" so enthusiastically that she had to hush her audience to get on with her speech. Harris's field operation—calling and texting voters, knocking on doors—was benefiting from the intense ground-level electoral engagement provoked by Clinton's loss in 2016. Activists, including many inspired to get into politics by the 2017 Women's March, worked steadily to spread her message and diligently lift the Democrats' poll numbers not just for the presidential race, but for House and Senate races too. Harris raised an unprecedented $1 billion and engaged hundreds of thousands of volunteers in record time.

Meanwhile, Trump amped up an already racist, misogynistic campaign, leading events likened to Nazi rallies filled with cries in support of mass deportation of immigrants, where one speaker called Puerto Rico a "floating island of garbage," and another called Harris the anti-Christ. Trump promised to be a protector of women, and added menacingly "whether the women like it or not," revealing his vow for what it really was: a threat.

By Election Day, the race was a toss-up. Harris's round-the-clock campaigning had boosted the Democrats' poll numbers to within striking distance of a win. Surveys of voters showed an extremely tight race, but most Harris supporters were optimistic. Trump was a convicted felon, had been found liable in court for sexual abuse, and had inspired and supported a violent insurrection to overturn the election results after his loss of the presidential race in 2020. He rambled incoherently and didn't put forth policy that would help anyone other than his billionaire backers, and even his supporters streamed out of his rallies early. Surely, the country was ready, as Harris often told her crowds, for a "new generation of leadership," and to "turn the page" from Trump's exhausting and perilous form of chaos.

And yet, once again, faced with the choice between all that and a talented, accomplished, intelligent, bridge-building, groundbreaking woman, America chose Trump.

In the face of a devastating defeat in which it appeared half of white women had again voted for Trump, and with every political commentator in possession of a suit jacket asserting their surety of what had gone wrong, the last thing anyone wanted to hear about was the same activism that had marked the period after Hillary Clinton's shocking loss in 2016.

Yet on the morning after the election, Congresswoman Alexandria Ocasio-Cortez, who had just been reelected to her fourth term in Congress, woke up and got on Instagram Live, looking exhausted but determined as she took stock of what had just happened. Less than twenty-four hours after the race had been called, a friend in Maine, who had worked nonstop during the election and whom I expected to be holed up nursing her wounds somewhere, instead forwarded me an invitation to a virtual event about the work to come. Six thousand people were on the call. "They're telling us, 'Focus, this is real, and we have to organize now. Pull it together,'" she told me.

That Thursday, a call cohosted by Indivisible and the Working Families Party drew more than 137,000 people. "That went for hours," said Fatima Goss Graves, the director of the National Women's Law Center. "I don't think I spoke until 10 p.m., and people stayed on and attendance grew. People are seeking not only community but ways to engage."

As election results came in, I'd been texting miserably with Amanda Litman. She hoped, she'd said, that her organization could carry on doing consequential work "even without a resistance 2.0, which I do not expect to see." Seven days later, seven thousand people had signed up with Run for Something, seven times the number it had drawn the week it launched on Trump's first Inauguration Day. "I was shocked, to be honest," said Litman. "I'm so glad to be wrong." Less than two weeks after Trump was inaugurated, as he enacted massive cuts to the federal government, openly rooting out those who worked on any initiatives tied to racial and gender diversity, Run for Something had drawn a jaw-dropping 27,000 candidates who had signed up to run at state, local, and federal levels, close to double the number of candidates Run For Something had supported in 2017 and 2018—both historic years for a new generation of candidate—combined. It was one of the darkest periods in American history, and yet there was reason for engagement on the horizon.

Throughout her presidential campaign, Kamala Harris often said, "When we fight, we win." After her election loss, she added a crucial footnote. "But here's the thing: Sometimes the fight takes a while. That doesn't mean we won't win." While the guys on television were expressing their Big Feelings about everything everyone had done wrong and the bleak future we faced because of it, the women I was seeing on Zoom screens looked flinty and knowing, like they had simply vomited and slept and were now ready to discuss legal, medical, electoral, and fundraising strategies.

"This story for us doesn't end with we lost that one time and gave up," said Goss Graves, who is also a civil rights lawyer. "That is just not how the story ends. This is a particularly tough period in our nation's history but it's actually not the worst period for Black folks or for women in this country. I don't want to sound glib when I say this, but I never thought the fight for our freedom would be easily secured or durable without further fight."

"The muscle memory has kicked back in as the grief and shock has worn off," Litman told me. "It feels more clear-eyed about how hard this will be. But there is also a history of winning against him." She added, "This time we can all jump right in without building the plane while we fly it."

The resistance is dead. Long live the resistance?

Conclusion

Men literally have no idea how to even legitimately recognize or name our anger—largely because we don't either. This is new territory for everybody. Women's rage has been so sublimated for so long that there's simply no frame for what happens when it finally comes to the surface.

—*Sara Robinson*

In an essay about how devastated she had been by the 2016 election, as a dedicated member of Hillary Clinton's campaign staff, Amanda Litman described how she had moved forward, founding Run for Something, one of the most successful new political organizations in the country.

"My anger is my cup of coffee in the morning," she wrote. "It gets me out of bed and keeps me focused. . . . Simply doing the damn thing has soothed me and brought me back to myself. Every memo I write, every donor I meet with, every reporter I speak to, each conversation I have, is guided by strategy but fueled by the fury I feel at my country, at dangerous men, at my party, and at the very system of democracy I love that painfully let me down."

When I first read these words after the 2016 election, I was already thinking a lot about the role of fury in politics. Once I dove in and started studying and writing about women's anger, I realized that those months had been one of the physically healthiest periods of my adulthood. As Litman had described her own experience, there had been something about spending my days and nights immersed in anger—mine and the anger of others—that had been undeniably good for me.

It seemed to fly in the face of everything I had ever been taught about fury's ill effects on the human body, things I had believed to be true on some level even as I had begun to write this book. "It's bad for them," my dentist told me, shaking his head sadly, of all the angry women he had treated since the 2016 election. "They grind their teeth."

Yes, I wanted to reclaim and excavate the value in women's anger, I had written in an early draft, but I also understood the emotion to have other, damaging dimensions, the ones that had been affirmed to me so often by culture, by my sources, that I had absorbed as truth. What I wrote when I started this book was that while anger might be politically useful, activating, thrilling, I knew that too much of it was *also* bad for you . . . poisonous, internally damaging.

By the time I completed the manuscript, I no longer believed that anger was harmful. In fact, I returned again and again to a proclamation made by Elizabeth Cady Stanton, nearly two centuries earlier, about the dangers of holding anger in: "If women would indulge more freely in vituperation, they would enjoy ten times the health they do. It seems to me they are suffering from repression."

My health had not been improved simply by my ability to let loose my ire; it had also been the chance to take seriously *other* women's rage, the fact that I'd been forced—encouraged—to really examine those emotions that we spend so much of our lives being told to avoid or look away from or laugh at. Writing this book had permitted me to stare straight at them, to think hard about them and consider the credit they deserve for shaping the nation.

I confess that I am now suspicious of nearly every attempt to code anger as unhealthy, no matter how well meaning or persuasive the source. I believe that Stanton was correct: What is bad for women, when it comes to anger, are the messages that cause us to bottle it up, let it stew, keep it silent, feel shame and isolation for ever having felt it or rechannel it in inappropriate directions. What is good for us is opening our mouths and letting it out, permitting ourselves to feel it and say it and think it and act on it and integrate it into our lives, just as we integrate joy and sadness and worry and optimism.

I had been given a gift: the opportunity to explore the dimensions and be curious about and respectful of my own anger, as well as the rage of other women. It felt *great*. *I* felt great. In getting to voice and appreciate fury, I had found relief, release, inspiration, and exhilaration.

But I was also aware that my experience was unusual, that it could not be advice that might apply to others. So while sure, I urge those who can comfortably do so to scream, yell, curse, write it out, phone a friend, and not keep themselves from *feeling* their own anger, you will find here no call to lean into your own rage as I have into mine.

I was not paying any price for expressing my ire, in fact I was *being paid* for it; it was my work, my job to take women's anger seriously. My editors, bosses, friends were taking this project, and therefore the fury it was unpacking, seriously. It was glorious. But I can't tell women to express their anger as I have and not acknowledge that in the real world, this rage might get them fired, deny them raises and promotions, or invite punishments and violence. We live in a world in which a Black woman, angry at being pulled over for no reason, risks arrest, and a woman angry at being unjustly arrested risks death; in which young women are shot, or run down by cars, because they—or because another woman—have rejected the advances of a man.

Having had the rare and privileged experience of having had my anger taken seriously, valued on its merits, I no longer believe that it is *anger* that is hurting us, but rather the system that punishes us for expressing it, that doesn't respect or hear it, that isn't curious about it, that mocks or ignores it. *That's* what's making us sick; *that's* what's making us feel crazy, alone; *that's* why we're grinding our teeth at night. Women yearn for permission, and simultaneously hunger for someone to express any curiosity at all about what they might be feeling. "We get told all the time that our anger is disruptive, that it is a distraction, that it is not helpful, and that in fact it is divisive and moving us backwards," said Black Lives Matter cofounder Alicia Garza, adding angrily that no one ever wonders why we are so livid.

And so it is not women (or not *only* women) who must change our behaviors; it's the system built to suppress our ire, and thus our power, by design. We can change it by protesting and marching and calling and sending postcards to elected officials, by donating money and knocking on doors for candidates and running for office, and making demands of our government and in our schools, communities, and workplaces, on behalf of ourselves and, crucially, alongside and on behalf of those with more reason to be furious and less ability to use that fury than we have.

But more immediately, we can change it by doing what the world does *not* do: by acknowledging, paying attention to, respecting, and not shying away from *other* women's anger. Seek it out, notice it, ask women what makes them angry and then listen to them when they tell you. If part of what they're angry at is you, take it in, acknowledge how their frustrations might mirror your own, even if they are directed at you.

Consider that the white men are rarely told that *their* anger is bad for them. Rather, and correctly, we understand that what's bad for them are the conditions that have provoked their frustration: loss of jobs and stature, the shortage of affordable health care, day care, the scourge of drug addiction. We understand their anger to be politically instructive, to point us toward problems that must be addressed. What we all—in the media, and in politics, and in our personal lives—can try to do is to treat the anger of women as we treat the anger of white men. That also means considering its potential: understanding that the fury of contemporary women at inequity, at sexism and racism and lack of representation, is made of the very same stuff that founding father Thomas Paine's anger was when he wrote the words that inspired American colonists' fight for independence from Britain, and that the demands it prompts might be just as transformative. Rage birthed this nation—along with its baked-in inequities, the very limits against which members of its majority population are now furiously straining.

Consider what Catharine MacKinnon wrote in February of 2018, arguing that #metoo has made a kind of progress that decades of legal reforms had not: "It is . . . this uprising of the formerly disregarded . . . that is changing everything already . . . [T]oday's movement that is shifting gender hierarchy's tectonic plates." As our current political reality under a second Donald Trump regime proves, we must never underestimate the pushback to any shift that can be reasonably described as tectonic, something that moves and shakes the ground on which we stand. The desire to push disruptive social fury back down underground is strong. The rage must be stronger still to resist the pull of indifference and the scorn of the powerful.

Martin Luther King Jr. understood that as well as anyone, and it's what made him insist, in his most famous speech, that "this sweltering summer of the Negro's legitimate discontent will not pass until there is an invigorating autumn of freedom and equality. Nineteen-sixty-three is not an end, but a beginning. And those who hope that the Negro needed to blow off steam and will now be content will have a rude awakening if the nation returns to business as usual. . . . The whirlwinds of revolt will continue to shake the foundations of our nation until the bright day of justice emerges."

What King commanded we too must command: We must insist on our discontent, not permit it to be muffled or put behind us swiftly. We must emerge on its other side with substantive, real victories: changes in law, policy, representation, power, a remaking not only of rules to better support equality—via criminal justice and environmental reform, the expansion of reproductive justice, of workers' rights and strengthening of a social safety net—but a reformation of the very attitudes that have permitted inequality to be put into law again and again.

Repeatedly, I have been asked—of the Women's March, of #metoo, of women's drive toward elected office, of the post-*Dobbs* electoral victories for reproductive rights and access: "Is this a moment or a movement?" In part, the questioners craved reassurance that the hard work, difficult feelings, the fear and pain and risk of resistance, were in service of something big, long-term, and important.

But it is not an either-or. Because movements are made up of moments, strung out over months, years, decades, and many of those years, those decades, are characterized by brutal, sometimes dehumanizing regress. But the moments of progress become clear to us as movements—are made to look smooth like a straight line—only after they have made a substantive difference. It was nine years between Emmett Till's murder and the passing of the Civil Rights Act. It was more than eighty years between the first 1830s meeting of abolitionists and suffragists and the passage of the Nineteenth Amendment, more than 130 years before the passage of the Voting Rights Act. That law was recently weakened by the Supreme Court, a body that in 2018 also defended states' rights to kick voters off the voter registration lists, disproportionately targeting minority voters. Which means that the movement for full democratic voting rights in the United States is ongoing, two centuries since our independence. It's easy to feel defeated by this, but more worthwhile to instead feel inspired: to know that in resisting and dissenting today, we are playing our parts in a story with long, righteous, proud roots. *We* determine whether or not we change the world.

The task, even in dark days—especially in dark days—is to keep going, to not turn back, to not give in to the easier path, the one where we weren't angry all the time, where we accepted the comforts of racial and economic advantage that will always be on offer to those who don't challenge power. Our job is to stay angry . . . perhaps for a very long time.

"It is probably going to be years," teenager X González told reporters in 2018 about their battle against the gun lobby. "And at this point, I don't know that I mind. Nothing that's worth it is easy . . . We could very well die trying to do this. But we could very well die *not* trying to do this too. So why not die for something rather than nothing?"

González seemed to know in youth what it took some activists ages to figure out: The challenges ahead for them, for all of us, will be ever present, but they cannot stop us. Vivian Gornick has written of her initial delight, as a woman in the 1970s, discovering the writing of the first-wave feminists who had come before her by a century: "We were . . . reincarnating as the feminists of previous generations," she wrote. "I remember reading Elizabeth Cady Stanton and feeling amazed that a hundred years ago she had said exactly what I was now saying. Amazed, and gratified. Not sobered. That would come later."

What should have been sobering, of course—what was sobering to me reading Flo Kennedy and Audre Lorde and Gornick herself, ever more acutely daunting in the wake of the second Trump election, with its sweeping attacks on racial and gender integration protections—is that if women have been here before, yet we had to get here again, the process of change was going to be slow, hard, and often circular. As Gornick recalls of how she thought in the 1970s, "I began to see it was going to take longer than any of us had expected. Much longer."

It feels all the more discouraging to be writing this in the midst of a second Donald Trump administration in which the stated aims of the right-wing government are not just to eradicate all the progress made by the previous generations of angry fighters—from affirmative action and abortion rights to diversity initiatives and labor and environmental protections—but also to change all the rules of governance and civic participation, to wrest the power of checks and balances away from the Senate and House of Representatives, to build a Supreme Court that will do the bidding of the president. So many of the efforts of the Trump administration are to suppress the abilities of angry people to rise up through protest, agitation, organizing, and coalition building. But while this may seem to be a new chilling chapter in the country's history, it is in line with the many ways the most powerful in this country have worked to resist and punish the reforms of those with less power: by breaking unions, keeping people from voting, threatening violent retribution against those who challenged their authority.

At the start of 2025, I was comforted by historians who regularly reminded me that those who want a more equal and inclusive nation, in which more people live with dignity and stability and protections and rights, have been through worse, and started with fewer resources, than we have today. And it's worth noting that while Trump and his posse of arrogant, cruel, and unqualified minions possess the power now, their frenzied, haphazard use of it to shame and scare people from expressing dissent actually shows how weak they are, how little their agenda can stand up to challenge, how avidly they want to protect it from the masses, who they understand have the power to take them down.

But yes: This will be hard and punishing and will take a long time. And the fact is, that is the message being sent by those who want to quiet dissent: They want us to feel daunted and terrified and exhausted and hopeless more than they want us to feel mad. They want to drain us of our energies to fight, because they are afraid that if we fight, we might, once again—with time and extraordinary effort—win.

That it will take a long time shouldn't scare us. It should fortify us. It *must* fortify us, as it seems to fortify X González. And we should remember that with each imperfect, and eventually stalled, stage of major social change has come some real progress: expanded voting rights, increases in liberty for more kinds of people, greater bodily autonomy. And yes, after each step has come the siren song of not-anger—of complicity and satisfaction and loyalty to the traditional structures that soothed the burns left by the revolt. But it's nowhere near time for that yet.

We need to work to ensure that this moment will have spurred real change, to know that the changes we make will echo far into the future. Consider Shirley Chisholm, who cried when she was mad, and who didn't win. She lost. And yet. She pulled Barbara Lee into politics. Barbara Lee, who pioneered a bill in 2015 that would overturn the Hyde Amendment—a law that prohibits federal funding for abortions and thus puts abortion care out of reach especially for poor women—a major step forward for poor women on an issue that no one had dared to touch since the 1970s. Lee's bill went nowhere. But enthusiasm for her efforts would help opposition to Hyde find its way into the presidential agenda of Hillary Clinton. Who lost. And whose loss helped spur the entry of perhaps tens of thousands of women into electoral politics and provoked this country to take women's experiences of sexual harassment seriously for the first time. Some of those women will lose too. But that will not be the end of the story either. For those women propelled Kamala Harris into the vice presidency in 2020 and worked their hearts out for her presidential candidacy in 2024.

At all the marches, all the rallies, you'll see one sign over and over again. It is a Mexican proverb, apparently taken from the Greek: "They thought they could bury us; they didn't know we were seeds." Women's anger has been buried, over and over again. But it has seeded the ground; we are the green shoots of furies covered up long ago.

As the philosopher Myisha Cherry has argued, "I want to convince you that there are types of anger that are not bad." In particular, she is interested in anger at injustice, regarding it as a wholly appropriate response to inequity. "Here are some of the features of the anger at injustice: it recognizes wrongdoing. This recognition is not mistaken; this person is not delusional or making this up in their head. It is not selfish. So when someone is angry at injustice they're not just concerned with themselves but also other people . . . this anger does not violate other people's rights and most importantly, it desires change."

If you happen to be reading this in the future, having stumbled across it in an attempt to find out if you're allowed to be angry about whatever you're angry about, let me say: Yes. Yes, you are allowed. You are in fact obligated.

And if you're reading this now, in its moment, with me, if you've gotten to this page because you've been feeling rage at the unfairness and injustice and at the flaws of this country and because your anger is making you want to change your life in order to change the world, then I have something incredibly important to say: Don't forget how this feels.

Tell a friend, write it down, so you will remember. The future will come, ushered in by you. If we survive this, if we make it better—even just a little bit better, but I hope a lot better—the urgency will fade, perhaps the ire will calm, the relief will take you, briefly. And that's good, that's okay.

But then the world will come and tell you that you shouldn't get mad again, because you were kind of nuts and you yelled at the TV and weren't so pretty and life will be easier when you get fun again. And it will be awfully tempting to put away the pictures of yourself from a rally, to stuff your protest signs in the attic, and to slink back, away from the raw bite of fury, to ease back into whatever new reality is made after whatever advances we achieve now.

But I say to all the women and girls reading this now, and to my future self: What you're angry about now—injustice—will still exist, even if you yourself are not experiencing it, or are tempted to stop thinking about *how* you experience it, and how you contribute to it. Others are still experiencing it, still mad; some of them are mad at you. Don't forget them; don't write off their anger. Stay mad for them. Stay mad *with* them. They're right to be mad, and you're right to be mad alongside them.

Being mad is correct; being mad is American; being mad can be joyful and productive and connective. Don't *ever* let anyone talk you out of being mad.

Acknowledgments

One million thanks to the brilliant Ruby Shamir, who translated my voice and also somehow inhabited my brain. And to Kendra Levin, who was patient and assured in her vision that this could be a book that might work for young people. I am so grateful to my agent, Elyse Cheney, who made this thing I'd been imagining might happen *actually* happen.

Thank you to Sarah Creech and Adara Sánchez Anguiano, whose cover design and illustration blew us all away, and to everyone at S&S Children's, including Amanda Brenner, Brian Luster, Tom Daly, Chava Wolin, Tionne Townsend, and all those in marketing and publicity who will help this book find its way.

My deepest gratitude is to those who spoke with me about their experiences and perspectives, now many decades younger than I. We didn't know when we decided to make a young readers edition of *Good and Mad* that it would be published in a political context in which the state would be working so brazenly to destroy the systems that encourage critical thinking, education, historical critique, and analysis. I think often about how writing the first version of this book involved learning so much history I had never been taught, even in the best of times; transforming it has reminded me of the future I have yet to see, and the children of today—and tomorrow—who will be fighting tooth and nail not just to wrest back the opportunities that are being taken from them but to expand the world, to make it more just and equitable for more people.

Selected Bibliography

For all my writing, I rely on a wide range of sources: books by historians and experts; public events and statements made by the people I'm writing about; the reporting of other journalists in print, on social media, on television, and in film; public policy research institutions; and my own original interviews with people.

This book relied on a *huge* range of these sources, and you'll notice that in some cases, I included a reference to my source within the sentence or paragraph in which I cited it. Much of the material in this book is based on articles I wrote for my adult books, *Big Girls Don't Cry*, *All the Single Ladies*, and *Good and Mad*, and many of my other sources have been accumulated in my reporting for *New York* magazine, the *New Republic*, *Salon*, the *New York Times Magazine*, and elsewhere.

You can find full lists of my sources in my original adult books, but below I'd like to highlight an incomplete selection of the resources that were fundamental to this book.

Alexander, Kerri Lee. "Elizabeth Freeman." National Women's History Museum, 2019. https://www.womenshistory.org/education-resources/biographies/elizabeth-freeman.

Baxandall, Rosalyn, and Linda Gordon, eds. *America's Working Women: A Documentary History, 1600 to the Present*. Rev. ed. W. W. Norton, 1995.

Beard, Mary. *Women and Power: A Manifesto.* Liveright, 2017.

Beauchamp, Keith, dir. *The Untold Story of Emmett Louis Till.* 2005. Posted November 20, 2012, by Mamie Till Mobley. YouTube, 1 hr., 8 min., 18 sec. https://www.youtube.com/watch?v=bvijYSJtkQk.

Betsey. "A Letter About Old Maids." *Lowell Offering*, October 1840. https://www2.cs.arizona.edu/patterns/weaving/periodicals/lo_40_10.pdf.

Brookhiser, Richard. "The Happy Medium." Review of *Other Powers: The Age of Suffrage, Spiritualism, and the Scandalous Victoria Woodhull*, by Barbara Goldsmith, and *Notorious Victoria: The Life of Victoria Woodhull, Uncensored*, by Mary Gabriel. *New York Times*, March 29, 1998. https://archive.nytimes.com/www.nytimes.com/books/98/03/29/reviews/980329.29brookht.html.

Burga, Solcyré. "How Four Trans Teens Threw the Prom of Their Dreams." *Time*, May 22, 2023. https://time.com/6281601/trans-teens-prom-capitol.

Butcher, Amy. "MIA: The Liberal Men We Love." *Literary Hub*, February 27, 2018. https://lithub.com/mia-the-liberal-men-we-love.

Capron, E. W. "Women's Rights Convention." *National Reformer*, August 3, 1848.

Carmon, Irin, and Amy Brittain. "Eight Women Say Charlie Rose Sexually Harassed Them—with Nudity, Groping and Lewd Calls." *Washington Post*, November 20, 2017. https://www.washingtonpost.com/investigations/eight-women-say-charlie-rose-sexually-harassed-them--with-nudity-groping-and-lewd-calls/2017/11/20/9b168de8-caec-11e7-8321-481fd63f174d_story.html.

CBS New York. "'We Stand on the Shoulders of Shirley Chisholm': Brooklyn Political Powerhouse Serves as Source of Inspiration for Sen. Kamala Harris." August 12, 2020. https://www.cbsnews.com/newyork/news/kamala-harris-shirley-chisholm.

Center for American Women and Politics. "Women in Elective Office 2025." Eagleton Institute of Politics, Rutgers University–New Brunswick, 2025. https://cawp.rutgers.edu/facts/current-numbers/women-elective-office-2025.

Chambers-Schiller, Lee Virginia. *Liberty, a Better Husband: Single Women in America; The Generations of 1780–1840.* Yale University Press, 1984.

Cherry, Myisha. "Anger Is Not a Bad Word." TEDxUofIChicago, May 21, 2015. YouTube, 17 min., 45 sec. https://www.youtube.com/watch?v=uysTk2EIotw.

Clinton, Hillary. Interview by Rachel Martin. *Morning Edition*, NPR, September 12, 2017. https://www.npr.org/2017/09/12/549430064/transcript-hillary-clinton-s-full-interview-with-npr-s-rachel-martin.

Coates, Ta-Nehisi. "Frederick Douglass: 'A Women's Rights Man.'" *Atlantic*, September 30, 2011. https://www.theatlantic.com/personal/archive/2011/09/frederick-douglass-a-womens-rights-man/245977.

Collins, Gail. *America's Women: Four Hundred Years of Dolls, Drudges, Helpmates, and Heroines*. Paperback ed. Perennial, 2004.

Collins, Gail. *When Everything Changed: The Amazing Journey of American Women from 1960 to the Present*. Little, Brown, 2009.

Coontz, Stephanie. *A Strange Stirring: The Feminine Mystique and American Women at the Dawn of the 1960s*. Basic Books, 2011.

Coontz, Stephanie. *Marriage, a History: From Obedience to Intimacy, or How Love Conquered Marriage*. Viking, 2005.

Coontz, Stephanie. "Marriage: Saying 'I Don't.'" *Los Angeles Times*, January 19, 2012. https://www.latimes.com/opinion/la-xpm-2012-jan-19-la-oe-coontz-marriage-20120119-story.html.

Cott, Nancy F. *Public Vows: A History of Marriage and the Nation*. Harvard University Press, 2000.

Cott, Nancy F. *The Bonds of Womanhood: "Woman's Sphere" in New England, 1780–1835*. 2nd ed. Yale University Press, 1997.

Deitcher, David, ed. *The Question of Equality: Lesbian and Gay Politics in America Since Stonewall*. Scribner, 1995.

Deshong, Travis. "Diane Nash: An Activist's Lessons for a New Generation." *Yale Daily News*, January 27, 2017. https://yaledailynews.com/blog/2017/01/27/diane-nash-an-activists-lessons-for-a-new-generation.

DiAngelo, Robin. "White Fragility." *International Journal of Critical Pedagogy* 3, no. 3 (2011): 54–70. https://janeway.uncpress.org/ijcp/article/id/643.

Dittmar, Kelly. "What You Need to Know About the Record Numbers of Women Candidates in 2020." Center for American Women and Politics, Eagleton Institute of Politics, Rutgers University–New Brunswick, August 10, 2025. https://cawp.rutgers.edu/blog/what-you-need-know-about-record-numbers-women-candidates-2020.

Donnella, Leah. "At the Sacred Stone Camp, Tribes and Activists Join Forces to Protect the Land." *Code Switch* (blog). NPR, September 10, 2016. https://www.npr.org/sections/codeswitch/2016/09/10/493110892.

Dubler, Ariela R. "In the Shadow of Marriage: Single Women and the Legal Construction of the Family and the State." *Yale Law Journal* 112, no. 7 (2003): 1641–1715. http://dx.doi.org/10.2307/3657498.

Ephron, Nora. "Women." *Esquire*, November 1, 1972. https://classic.esquire.com/article/1972/11/1/women-2.

Faludi, Susan. "The Patriarchs Are Falling. The Patriarchy Is Stronger Than Ever." *New York Times*, December 28, 2017. https://www.nytimes.com/2017/12/28/opinion/sunday/patriarchy-feminism-metoo.html.

Ferraro, Susan. "The Prime of Pat Schroeder." *New York Times Magazine*, July 1, 1990. https://www.nytimes.com/1990/07/01/magazine/the-prime-of-pat-schroeder.html.

Flanagan, Caitlin. "The Conversation #MeToo Needs to Have." *Atlantic*, January 29, 2018. https://www.theatlantic.com/politics/archive/2018/01/the-right-conversation-for-metoo/551732.

Foster, Frances Smith. *'Til Death or Distance Do Us Part: Love and Marriage in African America*. Oxford University Press, 2010.

Fought, Leigh. *Women in the World of Frederick Douglass*. Oxford University Press, 2017.

Friedan, Betty. *The Feminine Mystique*. 20th anniv. ed. Laurel Books, 1983.

Gay, Roxane. "Fifty Years Ago, Protesters Took on the Miss America Pageant and Electrified the Feminist Movement." *Smithsonian*, January 2018. https://www.smithsonianmag.com/history/fifty-years-ago-protestors-took-on-miss-america-pageant-electrified-feminist-movement-180967504.

Giddings, Paula. *When and Where I Enter: The Impact of Black Women on Race and Sex in America*. Bantam Books, 1984.

Ginzberg, Lori D. *Elizabeth Cady Stanton: An American Life.* Farrar, Straus and Giroux, 2009.

Goldstein, Dana. *The Teacher Wars: A History of America's Most Embattled Profession.* Doubleday, 2014.

Gornick, Vivian. "Who Says We Haven't Made a Revolution? A Feminist Takes Stock." *New York Times Magazine*, April 15, 1990. https://www.nytimes.com/1990/04/15/magazine/who-says-we-haven-t-made-a-revolution-a-feminist-takes-stock.html.

Gould, Stephen Jay. *The Mismeasure of Man*. Rev. ed. W. W. Norton, 1996.

Grundhauser, Eric. "The Great Harvard Pee-In of 1973." *Atlas Obscura*, December 23, 2016. https://www.atlasobscura.com/articles/the-great-harvard-peein-of-1973.

Guy-Sheftall, Beverly, ed. *Words of Fire: An Anthology of African-American Feminist Thought*. New Press, 1995.

Hamlin, Kimberly A. "Bathing Suits and Backlash: The First Miss America Pageants, 1921–1927." In *"There She Is, Miss America": The Politics of Sex, Beauty, and Race in America's Most Famous Pageant*, edited by Elwood Watson and Darcy Martin. Palgrave Macmillan, 2004.

Hanger, Kimberly S. "'The Fortunes of Women in America': Spanish New Orleans's Free Women of African Descent and Their Relations with Slave Women." In *Discovering the Women in Slavery: Emancipating Perspectives on the American Past*, edited by Patricia Morton. University of Georgia Press, 1996.

Harris-Perry, Melissa. "Women Are Angrier Than Ever Before—and They're Doing Something About It." *Elle*, March 9, 2018. https://www.elle.com/culture/career-politics/a19297903/elle-survey-womens-anger-melissa-harris-perry.

Hartmann, Margaret. "What Happened to the 20 Women Who Accused Trump of Sexual Misconduct." *Intelligencer*, February 26, 2019. https://nymag.com/intelligencer/2017/12/what-happened-to-trumps-16-sexual-misconduct-accusers.html.

Hoose, Phillip. *Claudette Colvin: Twice Toward Justice*. Melanie Kroupa Books, 2009.

Hoose, Phillip. *We Were There, Too! Young People in U.S. History*. Melanie Kroupa Books, 2001.

Israel, Betsy. *Bachelor Girl: 100 Years of Breaking the Rules—a Social History of Living Single*. Paperback ed. Perennial, 2003.

Jamison, Leslie. "I Used to Insist I Didn't Get Angry. Not Anymore." *New York Times Magazine*, January 17, 2018. https://www.nytimes.com/2018/01/17/magazine/i-used-to-insist-i-didnt-get-angry-not-anymore.html.

Katznelson, Ira. *When Affirmative Action Was White: An Untold History of Racial Inequality in Twentieth-Century America*. W. W. Norton, 2005.

Kessler-Harris, Alice. *Out to Work: A History of Wage-Earning Women in the United States.* 20th anniv. ed. Oxford University Press, 2003.

Khan-Cullors, Patrisse. "We Didn't Start a Movement. We Started a Network." *Medium*, February 23, 2016. https://medium.com/@patrissemariecullorsbrignac/we-didn-t-start-a-movement-we-started-a-network-90f9b5717668.

Laiz, Jana and Ann-Elizabeth Barnes. *"A Free Woman on God's Earth": The True Story of Elizabeth "Mumbet" Freeman, the Slave Who Won Her Freedom*. Crow Flies Press, 2009.

Life. "Mother Bloor: U.S. Communist Heroine." July 26, 1937.

Litman, Amanda. "I Wake Up and Go to Sleep Angry—and That's a Good Thing." *Women's Health*, October 17, 2017. https://www.womenshealthmag.com/life/a19948724/amanda-litman-run-for-something.

Lorde, Audre. "The Uses of Anger: Women Responding to Racism." Keynote presentation, National Women's Studies Association Conference, Storrs, CT, June 1981. BlackPast.org, August 12, 2012. https://www.blackpast.org/african-american-history/1981-audre-lorde-uses-anger-women-responding-racism.

Lovett, Laura L. *Conceiving the Future: Pronatalism, Reproduction, and the Family in the United States, 1890–1938*. University of North Carolina Press, 2007.

MacKinnon, Catharine A. "#MeToo Has Done What the Law Cannot." *New York Times*, February 4, 2018. https://www.nytimes.com/2018/02/04/opinion/metoo-law-legal-system.html.

May, Elaine Tyler. *Barren in the Promised Land: Childless Americans and the Pursuit of Happiness*. Harvard University Press, 1995.

May, Elaine Tyler. *Homeward Bound: American Families in the Cold War Era*. 2nd ed. Basic Books, 1999.

McGuire, Danielle L. *At the Dark End of the Street: Black Women, Rape, and Resistance—a New History of the Civil Rights Movement from Rosa Parks to the Rise of Black Power.* Alfred A. Knopf, 2010.

Moran, Rachel F. "How Second-Wave Feminism Forgot the Single Woman." *Hofstra Law Review* 33, no. 1 (2004). https://scholarlycommons.law.hofstra.edu/hlr/vol33/iss1/5.

Mukhopadhyay, Samhita. "2017: The Year Women's Anger Was Unleashed." *Mic*, December 22, 2017. https://www.mic.com/articles/187016/2017-the-year-womens-anger-was-unleashed.

National Woman Suffrage Association. "Declaration of Rights of the Women of the United States." In *The Selected Papers of Elizabeth Cady Stanton and Susan B. Anthony*. Vol. 3, *National Protection for National Citizens, 1873 to 1880*, edited by Ann D. Gordon. Rutgers University Press, 2003.

New York Times. "Death of Fred Douglass." February 21, 1895. https://archive.nytimes.com/www.nytimes.com/learning/general/onthisday/bday/0207.html.

Norton, Mary Beth. *Founding Mothers and Fathers: Gendered Power and the Forming of American Society*. Alfred A. Knopf, 1996.

Norton, Mary Beth. *Liberty's Daughters: The Revolutionary Experience of American Women, 1750–1800*. Cornell Paperbacks, 1996.

Olson, Lynne. *Freedom's Daughters: The Unsung Heroines of the Civil Rights Movement from 1830 to 1970*. Scribner, 2001.

Oluo, Ijeoma. "Does This Year Make Me Look Angry?" *Elle*, January 11, 2018. https://www.elle.com/culture/career-politics/a15063942/ijeoma-oluo-women-and-rage-2018.

Orleck, Annelise. "Clara Lemlich Shavelson." *Shalvi/Hyman Encyclopedia of Jewish Women*. Jewish Women's Archive, March 20, 2009. https://jwa.org/encyclopedia/article/shavelson-clara-lemlich.

Orleck, Annelise. *Rethinking American Women's Activism.* Routledge, 2015.

PBS. "Stop ERA." *Not Done: Women Remaking America.* February 26, 2013. Video, 10 min., 39 sec. https://www.pbs.org/video/makers-women-who-make-america-stop-era.

Peiss, Kathy. *Cheap Amusements: Working Women and Leisure in Turn-of-the-Century New York.* Temple University Press, 1986.

Penny, Laurie. "We're Not Done Here." *Longreads,* January 18, 2018. https://longreads.com/2018/01/18/were-not-done-here.

Peoples, Angela. "Don't Just Thank Black Women. Follow Us." *New York Times*, December 16, 2017. https://www.nytimes.com/2017/12/16/opinion/sunday/black-women-leadership.html.

Press, Joy. "The Life and Death of a Radical Sisterhood." *Cut*, November 15, 2017. https://www.thecut.com/2017/11/an-oral-history-of-feminist-group-new-york-radical-women.html.

Richards, Cecile. *Make Trouble: Standing Up, Speaking Out, and Finding the Courage to Lead.* With Lauren Peterson. Touchstone, 2018.

Roosevelt, Theodore. "Before the Mother's Conference." In *A Compilation of the Messages and Speeches of Theodore Roosevelt, 1901–1905*, edited by Alfred Henry Lewis. Bureau of National Literature and Art, 1906.

Schappes, Morris U. "Remembering the Waistmakers General Strike, 1909." *Jewish Currents*, May 3, 2015. https://jewishcurrents.org/remembering-the-waistmakers-general-strike-1909.

Scutts, Joanna, Sarah Gordon, and Valerie Paley. *Hotbed.* New York Historical, November 3, 2017–March 25, 2018.

Shepherd, Katie, Rachel Roubein, and Caroline Kitchener. "1 in 3 American Women Have Already Lost Abortion Access. More Restrictive Laws Are Coming." *Washington Post*, August 22, 2022. https://www.washingtonpost.com/nation/2022/08/22/more-trigger-bans-loom-1-3-women-lose-most-abortion-access-post-roe.

Smith, Mychal Denzel. "The Rebirth of Black Rage." *Nation*, August 13, 2015. https://www.thenation.com/article/archive/the-rebirth-of-black-rage.

Smithsonian National Museum of the American Indian. "Treaties Still Matter: The Dakota Access Pipeline." Accessed June 4, 2025. https://americanindian.si.edu/nk360/plains-treaties/dapl.cshtml.

Spruill Wheeler, Marjorie, ed. *One Woman, One Vote: Rediscovering the Woman Suffrage Movement*. NewSage Press, 1995.

Stein, Leon, ed. *Out of the Sweatshop: The Struggle for Industrial Democracy.* Quadrangle/New York Times Book Co., 1977.

Stoynoff, Natasha. "Physically Attacked by Donald Trump: A *People* Writer's Own Harrowing Story." *People*, October 12, 2016. https://people.com/politics/donald-trump-attacked-people-writer.

Streitmatter, Rodger. *Mightier Than the Sword: How the News Media Have Shaped American History.* 4th ed. Routledge, 2018.

Sugrue, Thomas J. *Sweet Land of Liberty: The Forgotten Struggle for Civil Rights in the North*. Random House Trade Paperbacks, 2009.

Thomas, Tess. "Tokata Iron Eyes on Why the Climate Movement Needs to Listen to Indigenous Voices." *Assembly* (blog). Malala Fund, November 18, 2020. https://assembly.malala.org/stories/tokata-iron-eyes-on-why-the-climate-movement-needs-to-listen-to-indigenous-voices.

Triece, Mary E. *On the Picket Line: Strategies of Working-Class Women During the Depression*. University of Illinois Press, 2007.

Tuck, Stephen. *We Ain't What We Ought to Be: The Black Freedom Struggle from Emancipation to Obama*. Belknap Press of Harvard University Press, 2011.

Twohey, Megan, and Michael Barbaro. "Two Women Say Donald Trump Touched Them Inappropriately." *New York Times*, October 12, 2016. https://www.nytimes.com/2016/10/13/us/politics/donald-trump-women.html.

Twohey, Megan, Jodi Kantor, Susan Dominus, Jim Rutenberg, and Steve Eder. "Weinstein's Complicity Machine." *New York Times*, December 5, 2017. https://www.nytimes.com/interactive/2017/12/05/us/harvey-weinstein-complicity.html.

Vapnek, Lara. *Breadwinners: Working Women and Economic Independence, 1865–1920*. University of Illinois Press, 2009.

Welter, Barbara. "The Cult of True Womanhood: 1820–1860." *American Quarterly* 18, no. 2, part 1 (1966): 151–174. https://doi.org/10.2307/2711179.

The Young Lady's Book: A Manual of Elegant Recreations, Exercises, and Pursuits. London: Vizetelly, Branston, 1829. https://archive.org/details/youngladysbooka00ladygoog/mode/2up.